animal
heroes

Also by David Long

Spectacular Vernacular: London's 100 Most Extraordinary
Buildings

Tunnels, Towers and Temples: London's 100 Strangest Places

Hidden City: The Secret Alleys, Courts and Yards of London's
Square Mile

Murders of London: In the Steps of the Capital's Killers

The Little Book of London

The Little Book of London Underground

London Underground: Architecture, Design & History

When Did Big Ben First Bong? 101 Crucial Questions about the
Greatest City on Earth

Blood, Sweat and Tyres: The Little Book of Motoring

Classic Cars

English Country House Eccentrics

English Eccentrics and their Bizarre Behaviour

animal
heroes

DAVID LONG

arrow books

Previously published as *The Animals' VC*

Published by Arrow 2013

2 4 6 8 10 9 7 5 3 1

First published in Great Britain in 2012 by Preface Publishing

Random House, 20 Vauxhall Bridge Road,
London SW1V 2SA

www.randomhouse.co.uk

Addresses for companies within The Random House Group Limited
can be found at: www.randomhouse.co.uk

The Random House Group Limited Reg. No. 954009

A CIP catalogue record for this book
is available from the British Library

ISBN 9780099574347

The Random House Group Limited supports the Forest Stewardship
Council® (FSC®), the leading international forest-certification organisation.
Our books carrying the FSC label are printed on FSC®-certified paper.
FSC is the only forest-certification scheme supported by the leading
environmental organisations, including Greenpeace. Our paper procurement
policy can be found at www.randomhouse.co.uk/environment

Typeset in Goudy by Palimpsest Book Production Ltd, Falkirk, Stirlingshire

Printed and bound by CPI Group (UK) Ltd, Croydon, CR0 4YY

Contents

For All the Unsung Heroes

Foreword

As well as its vital work treating the pets of people in need, PDSA has a long and proud tradition of recognising the bravery and devotion of animals in times of conflict. From pigeons flying behind enemy lines in World War II to Army dogs sniffing out explosive devices in Afghanistan, the charity has rightly drawn our attention to the life-saving deeds of our four-legged and feathered friends.

Commemorating the feats of 'those who also serve' is a valuable reminder that, no matter how sophisticated we become, there are some things that technology can never do as accurately and efficiently as these humble and noble creatures. It is fitting that we remember them in this way, and I hope this book, like the PDSA Dickin Medal itself, succeeds in raising the status of all animals in our society.

Paul O'Grady
Friend of the PDSA

Introduction: PDSA, the Allied Forces Mascot Club and the PDSA Dickin Medal

As People's Dispensary for Sick Animals was established during the Great War to address one serious aspect of the growing problem of poverty in London's East End it was perhaps inevitable that the initiative for the Allied Forces Mascot Club in the next war should have come from this same pioneering animal charity.

From its base in central London the club – unusual in that it had no human members – was created to recognise the increasingly important role being played by regimental and other service mascots. The membership as such included quite a motley collection of dogs, goats, birds, monkeys and at least one fox. Before long it expanded to accommodate many other service animals whose more specialised training saw them working alongside men and women on the home and battle fronts, out at sea and eventually even deep into enemy-held territory.

Having decided to acknowledge these animals' valuable contribution in this way, in 1943 the club took the natural step of honouring them too. Most obviously this was done with the introduction of the PDSA Dickin Medal, the only award of its type instituted during World War II and one which was established with the authority of the War Office behind it and the full support of the Imperial War Museum.

It was named for the charity's founder, the animal welfare pioneer Maria Elisabeth Dickin CBE (1870–1951). A formidable social reformer in her time and extremely well connected, Mrs Dickin recognised that such an award – besides being a real and significant morale booster in terrible times – would also serve to highlight the important work being done by the PDSA at home and abroad and thus help boost much-needed contributions from donors.

From the first the medal quickly became known around the world as the Animals' VC, in part because even at the height of the war such awards were only rarely made, but also because the circumstances leading to an award being made were never anything less than truly exceptional. The Dickin Medal was also unique and remains so in that consideration can only be given to the presentation of the award following a nomination from a recognised authority – one of the three services, for example, the police or another law enforcement agency, or an accredited organisation such as the United Nations.

Again like the Victoria Cross the medal itself is deliberately sober in design, a simple but large and weighty garlanded bronze medallion bearing the simple legends 'For Gallantry' and 'We Also Serve'. It is worn suspended from a tricolour ribbon, with the dark green, brown and blue symbolising the three services and the sea, land and air in which they fight. (Early Victoria Crosses similarly sported a red ribbon for army recipients and a blue one for navy until the latter was abolished following the formation of the Royal Air Force in 1918.)

From its inception every member of the AFMC was entitled to a membership badge – something akin to a campaign or service medal for combatants – but the Dickin Medal was conceived from the start as something very special indeed, to recognise only the most outstanding examples of gallantry and devotion. Because of this, and while it has been awarded to a variety of horses, dogs, one cat and British and Allied birds who have seen action or engaged with the enemy in many different countries around the globe, a mere 63 medals have been struck in nearly 70 years.

The very first awards made were to birds, three carrier pigeons involved in locating downed aircrew by providing important clues as to their likely positions. These birds must be counted among the many hundreds of thousands of such creatures which, volunteered by their owners, provided Allied forces with the sort of fast and secure communications that genuinely saved lives. More recently medals have been presented to trained specialist dogs engaged in hunting arms and explosives in the Gulf and Afghanistan, and to those aiding the massive rescue and recovery operation in central New York which followed the shattering attacks of 9/11.

Wherever the animals served, the citations for all 63 medal recipients stand first and foremost as an appropriate and solemn monument to the animals themselves. Looking back, their stories also provide us with unique and vivid snapshots of their respective actions and the background of war or terror against which these were played out, and of course as such they prove by turns engaging and uplifting and, as often, sad and deeply moving.

This has not prevented people debating at length the very concept of courage or bravery when applied to an animal, particularly when for example it could be argued that a carrier pigeon does what it does by instinct rather than by deliberation. What can not be doubted, however, is the often critically important contribution these and other animals have made and continue to make on the front line and closer to home.

They do this not just by exercising the skills peculiar to their species but also by providing solace, genuine companionship and a morale-boosting presence which, when facing the very extremes of danger, men and women, both military and civilian, recognise and depend upon.

Thirty-two birds, twenty-seven dogs, three Metropolitan Police horses and Simon the ship's cat – the stories of all 63 recipients provide a fascinating insight into an aspect of war, one which has begun to be told only quite recently. Some may find the notion of the medal a touch eccentric, but these animals and their achievements are an important part of history and as such this book is a roll-call of names which need to be heard and remembered.

To their friends and supporters there was never any doubt that as individuals the animals deserved the recognition that the award of a Dickin Medal brought them. Consider too that each animal in this book is representative of scores, hundreds or even thousands of others: animal heroes whose service to humanity should never go unnoticed, and upon whom lives have depended and, on occasion, history itself can genuinely be said to have hinged.

Chapter 1

A Friend in Need: Keeping up Morale

Recruited in considerable numbers from dogs' homes during the war years – also from pet owners keen to contribute in some way to the war effort (and as often as not from those unable properly to feed their pets due to food rationing) – many thousands of animals were assigned by their new military masters to perform particular duties but in the heat of battle went on to play a far more valuable role.

Some, for example, were professionally schooled and trained for often very specific military tasks, such as minehunting, search and rescue or guard duties at sensitive military sites. Others were taken on as ships' mousers or as ceremonial regimental mascots. But while animals may have performed such important tasks very well and to the best of their abilities, many of the most heroic and most fondly remembered are today recalled more for the companionship that was forged in the long emergency of the war – that is, as genuine friends – than for any individual skills or duties.

That said, by the 1940s and the inception of the PDSA Dickin Medal, there was already nothing particularly new about soldiers keeping pets. For example in the Great War a pig rescued during the sinking of the German cruiser *Dresden* in March 1915 became something of a celebrity. Renamed Tirpitz, he was adopted as the mascot of HMS *Glasgow* for a year before being retired to Portsmouth's Whale Island Gunnery School and then eventually auctioned off (for pork, sadly) to raise money for the Red Cross. Tommies serving in the trenches on the Western Front and elsewhere similarly took on stray cats and dogs all the time, and indeed one of the latter – Thélus – was even fitted with a home-made wooden prosthetic by a brigade medical officer after losing his paw.

Elsewhere on the Western Front many rather more exotic creatures popped up in what was otherwise a most unpromising environment for animals. Places otherwise denuded of all traces of wildlife bar scavenging rats and the inevitable lice, the trenches were at different times enlived by several monkeys and at least one goat with a penchant for tobacco, who given the chance would snatch cigarettes from any Tommy unwise enough to come within range.

The best of these animals did far more than entertain the troops with their antics, however, most obviously by boosting morale in times of almost inconceivable stress and immense personal danger. Time and again, in researching the role of animals in war, one reads of animals who would ordinarily baulk or bolt from loud noises remaining calm during attacks; of horses, dogs and even cats, traditionally so aloof and detached, who remained by their handlers' sides in the midst of battle, showing real loyalty and courage as well as offering comfort and support to their comrades in arms.

Not infrequently this was done at great personal cost or when the animal in question was itself seriously wounded. In the heat of battle, behind enemy lines, on the home front and even in captivity their stories are rarely if ever less remarkable than those of the men and women who knew them – and they can be just as moving.

Judy
English Pointer
POW Camp, Medan, 1942–5
Date of Award: 2 May 1946
For magnificent courage and endurance in Japanese prison camps which helped to maintain morale among her fellow prisoners, and also for saving many lives through her intelligence and watchfulness.

The only canine ever officially listed as an Allied prisoner of war, this handsome liver and white pointer also enjoyed the distinction of being 'interviewed' as part of a special Victory Day BBC broadcast on 8 June 1946, when her barks were heard by many thousands of listeners around the country.

Born in Shanghai in 1937, Judy had served in the Royal Navy as ship's dog aboard two vessels, HMS *Gnat* and HMS *Grasshopper*. The last named took part in a number of actions during the Malay–Singapore campaign, and with Judy included in the ship's company *Grasshopper* headed for Java after the fall of Singapore. Attacked by Japanese fighter-bombers in February 1942, the ship was eventually forced to beach and subsequently blew up.

Judy, together with 75 crew, 50 passengers and sailors from a companion vessel HMS *Dragonfly*, found themselves marooned on Singkep, an inhospitable and apparently uninhabited island to the east of Sumatra, surrounded by oily, burning seawater with little in the way of food and no obvious source of drinking water. Despite repeated searches for a source which was safe to drink, no spring could be found until – after some determined digging at the shoreline – a bedraggled and oil-covered Judy was observed drinking from what turned out to be a safe, non-saline source. Able to refresh themselves from the same spring, the crews of the two ships were then fortunate enough to commandeer a passing Chinese junk and set sale for the north-east coast of Sumatra.

On 10 March, however, after a gruelling 200-mile overland trek towards Padang and less than three miles from safety, they found themselves surrounded while taking refuge in what turned out to be a Japanese-held village. Now prisoners of war, they were taken by open truck – with Judy hidden in the back beneath a stack of empty rice sacks – to the Gloergoer POW camp at Medan. It was here that she met Leading Aircraftman Frank Williams (1919–2006), remembered now as a tall gentle sort with a kind face beneath his dark wavy hair, who unhesitatingly shared with her his meagre ration of maggoty rice. Thus began what a fellow prisoner was later to describe as 'three to four years of the most horrific labour, torture, starvation and every degradation the Japanese could inflict on us'.

Over that period of captivity the two were clearly devoted to each other, Williams enjoying the companionship enormously but also valuing Judy's uncanny instinct and ability to alert him and his comrades to the presence of dangerous snakes and scorpions as well as aircraft. 'I remember thinking,' he noted many years later, 'what on earth is a beautiful English pointer like this doing here, with no one to care for her. I realised that even though she was thin, she was a survivor.' She also worked hard to keep the men's spirits high, with several being heard ruefully to observe that if the 'old bitch' could hang on for release, then so could they.

When the guards were administering punishment to the prisoners, Judy would repeatedly attempt to distract them by growling and barking, and on a number of occasions the worst of them threatened to shoot the dog dead if she did not back off. With such incidents becoming more heated, Williams was eventually able to secure her safety by holding out the promise of a puppy to the Japanese camp commandant. In exchange the commandant, frequently in his cups after too much saki, agreed to help by giving her official status – 'Prisoner No.81A Gloergoer, Medan' – thus providing her with a measure of security. (He got his puppy in the end too, with another one from Judy's litter of nine being smuggled into the adjacent internment camp occupied by Dutch women. Hidden in a basket of bananas and given a whiff of chloroform to keep it quiet, the puppy reportedly went on to fulfil a similar morale-raising role to its mother.)

In June 1944 the men in the camp were told they were being moved to a camp in Singapore, travelling aboard the SS *Van Warwyck*. Dogs were not permitted on board, but Williams refused to leave Judy behind and carried her up the gangway in a rice sack thrown over his shoulder, having previously trained her to lie still, upside down and without making any noise. With the Korean guards on the lookout for canine stowaways, Judy managed, incredibly, to lie still for three hours before Williams was able to stow her away out of sight in the ship's hold.

The conditions were horrendous, with more than 700 POWs squeezed into every available space, and on 26 June the ship was torpedoed and began to sink. There seemed to be no escape for the men in Williams's section, but he was able to push the dog through a porthole located 15 feet above the waterline. He did so in the hope that she would be able to swim to safety but had to face the possibility that he might himself drown.

In pitch dark and pinned down by wreckage, the men awaited their fate, but a second explosion blew a hole in the side of the ship enabling them to drop into the water. Unfortunately Judy by then had disappeared, Williams later recalling the expression on her face before she fell into the water which seemed to say, 'What is all this in aid of?'

After a couple of hours in the water Williams and his ship-mates were recaptured and sent to a new camp, but news soon reached him that, after leaping from the porthole, Judy had paddled around in the water retrieving pieces of debris to help other men keep afloat and had allowed others to hold on to her as she swam. It was to be another three days, however, before the two were united in a scene an officer described in a letter home as both joyous and touching. Decades later Williams recounted the moment himself to a reporter from the *Daily Mail*: 'I couldn't believe my eyes. As I entered the camp, a scraggy dog hit me square between the shoulders and knocked me over! I'd never been so glad to see the old girl. And I think she felt the same.'

The two were far from safe, however, as Williams was forced to face an even greater challenge, spending a year in the jungle laying railway tracks while subsisting on daily rations comprising of no more than a handful of rotten tapioca and some foul water. But here too Judy played a vital role, Williams insisting that her presence saved his and many other lives 'in so many ways. The greatest way . . . was giving me a reason to live. All I had to do was look at her and into those weary, bloodshot eyes and I would ask myself: What would happen to her if I died? I had to keep going. Even if it meant waiting for a miracle.'

There were joyful moments too, of course, with memories of Judy chasing monkeys, barking at flying foxes, burying a much-prized elephant bone and spooking the superstitious guards by running around the camp with an ancient Malay skull clamped in her jaws. Over this same period she survived a number of alligator bites, attacks from wild dogs and the feared Sumatran tiger, and many severe beatings from the guards, who came to loathe her. Perhaps fearing a prisoner rebellion, however, they never carried out their threats to shoot her dead and cook her. That said, a permanent scar beneath one eye bore witness to one of Judy's many close shaves during this time, and efforts were made to keep her hidden from the worst of the Japanese.

Despite her sterling service and official status, when the war against Japan was won, Judy still had to be smuggled aboard another ship – this time a troopship bound for Liverpool and the spiritual home she had never seen. Fortunately the troops were able to sneak her past the dock police, and once aboard they entrusted her to the care of the ship's cook so that she was relatively well fed during the voyage across the Mediterranean.

An unavoidable six months of quarantine followed, at Hackbridge in Surrey, and then in May 1946 in London's Cadogan Square, Judy – by now something of a heroine – was invited to London and enrolled as a member of the Returned British Prisoners of War Association, the only dog so honoured. Chairman of the association Major the Viscount Tarbut MC pinned a hard-won and well-deserved Dickin Medal on her collar, with PDSA at the same time honouring Frank Williams with the White Cross of St Giles for his strength, his fortitude and, it has to be said, his cunning in bringing this splendid animal through her ordeals and back with him to England.

For a year the pair spent much of their time visiting the

relatives of those prisoners who had not survived the war, Williams believing that Judy's presence was frequently a genuine comfort to the bereaved. In May 1948 he accepted a post with a government-funded food scheme in east Africa, and Judy naturally went with him. Very sadly, just two years later, she was found to have a tumour, and at the age of 13 she was put to sleep and buried beneath a large granite and marble memorial. This was built by Frank Williams himself, greatly saddened by the loss, and tells of their adventures together, Judy's outstanding courage and devotion and their quite remarkable relationship.

After Frank's death in 2006 the Dickin Medal and collar were presented to the Imperial War Museum in London to go on permanent display. Hoping that Judy's courage and devotion would be remembered by generations to come, Frank's widow Doris noted, 'although I never knew Judy in life, she always felt like a member of our family who undoubtedly and repeatedly saved my husband's life and that of his fellow prisoners during the war'.

Tich
Mongrel
North Africa and Italy, 1941–5
Date of Award: 1 July 1949
For loyalty, courage and devotion to duty under hazardous conditions of war, 1941 to 1945, while serving with the 1st King's Rifle Corps in North Africa and Italy.

Shown alongside the citations and artefacts of the regiment's 24 Victoria Cross recipients, the Dickin Medal on display at the regimental museum of the Royal Green Jackets (The Rifles) in Winchester was awarded to a black Egyptian mongrel called Tich. Nicknamed the Desert Rat, Tich was adopted by 1st Battalion, King's Royal Rifle Corps early on in the North Africa campaign, saw the victory at El Alamein and remained with them until the end of the war, serving with a carrier platoon all the way up through Italy.

By the early 1940s many service dogs at home and abroad were listed as members of PDSA's official Allied Forces Mascots Club, which recognised and promoted their roles as companions and working dogs. Many of these were well-disciplined animals professionally trained for specific tasks after being donated in response to official appeals for recruits. Many others, however, were the sort of scruffy unloved strays which servicemen occasionally adopt when on tour, or which tag along when troops are in town in the hope of a free meal, companionship and shelter.

Mostly terrier but it is thought with a bit of dachshund thrown in, Tich very definitely fell into the latter category: a good honest 'bitsa', with a friendly nature and strong character, but also something of a ruffian. Her good fortune after being adopted in 1941 was to catch the eye of Rifleman Thomas Walker a couple of years later, after which the two were rarely apart. While he and his comrades fought their way through Algeria and across the Mediterranean to take part in the invasion of southern Italy, Tich was routinely to be seen in the front line atop one of the platoon's caterpillar-tracked Bren universal carriers or on the bonnet of Walker's stretcher-bearing jeep.

Clearly she allowed herself some time off, however, and after being smuggled aboard a troopship for the crossing to Italy was found to be carrying a litter. In all Tich produced a total of 15 puppies, but was more often to be seen riding into battle, her presence on the Bren UC and a habit of what the battalion chaplain called 'howling like a wolf' being repeatedly referred to as a real morale booster by many of her two-legged comrades.

Unfortunately, sticking by her handler in this way – Walker was an exceptionally courageous soldier who was subsequently awarded the Military Medal for rescuing and treating injured soldiers while under heavy fire – meant Tich frequently found herself in danger. On a number of occasions she took hits, once being wounded seriously, when it was thought that the injuries to her head would finish her off. This at occurred at Faenza, during the push up through Italy, when Tich sustained a badly broken nose and multiple shrapnel wounds while taking part in Operation Olive against the Germans' Gothic Line. By no means as well known as the D-Day landings, the operation was nevertheless a mammoth undertaking – essentially the invasion from the southern flank of enemy-controlled Europe – and was by far the largest engagement on the Italian peninsula during the whole of the war.

With up to 1.2 million Allied soldiers launching themselves against Field Marshal Kesselring's last major line of defence, and the commander of Britain's Eighth Army comparing the scale and ferocity of the fighting to El Alamein and Monte Cassino, Rifleman Walker's duties meant that he and Tich repeatedly found themselves in an open vehicle in areas that were being heavily shelled and mortared. In particular they were involved in the rescue and evacuation of wounded members of the 43rd Indian (Ghurka) Lorried Infantry Brigade. In the absence of a medical officer Walker was detailed to man a regimental first aid post at one end of the front on the River Marzeno. Tich's indomitable spirit – undimmed even when she was injured – combined with Walker's calm efficiency to boost the spirits of the seriously wounded in what was clearly a perilous situation.

Throughout the heavy fighting Tich never left her post or ran for cover, and when news of the engagement reached England newspaper reports described her as the brave dog of 'an oustand-ingly brave man'. This assessment was subsequently echoed by Walker's commanding officer, Lieutenant Colonel. E. A. W. Williams, who described the dog's courage and devotion to duty as being of 'very real and considerable value. Her courageous example materially helped many men to keep their heads and sense of proportion in times of extreme danger.' The sight of her, he said, 'put heart in the men as she habitually rode on her master's jeep and refused to leave her post even when bringing in wounded under heavy fire'.

Eventually these words formed part of the official recommendation for a new Dickin Medal to be struck, and on 3 September 1949 – ten years after Britain entered the war against Germany – it was duly presented to Tich by Major Peter Earle MC on behalf of the colonel commandant of the 1st King's Royal Rifle Corps. The presentation formed part of the Animals' Rally organised by the *Star* newspaper at Wembley Stadium, when more than 8,000 members of the public turned out to see Tich and to hear the regimental chaplain describe a dog who would 'never eat or drink until ordered to do so'.

For the next ten years Tich enjoyed a happy retirement in Newcastle, she and ex-Rifleman Walker still inseparable and the two of them making frequent appearances in order to raise funds to continue the work of PDSA. When she died in 1959 Tich was laid to rest at the Ilford PDSA Animal Cemetery in east London. Her grave was still receiving visits from comrades of Rifleman Walker until a year or two ago, and in 2007 a bugler from Tich's old regiment sounded the last post following the restoration of the cemetery.

'Able Seaman' Simon
Cat
China, 1949
Date of Award: 11 December 1949 (posthumous)
Served on HMS *Amethyst* during the Yangtze Incident, disposing of many rats though wounded by shell blast. Throughout the

incident his behaviour was of the highest order, although the blast was capable of making a hole over a foot in diameter in a steel plate.

A raggedy and undernourished black and white tom picked for a ship's cat from the docks of Hong Kong's Stonecutter Island, Simon joined HMS *Amethyst* in 1948 when it passed through the Crown colony en route from Malaya. The stray was smuggled aboard the frigate by Ordinary Seaman George Hickinbottom, a 17-year-old crew member fortunate enough to have a cat lover for a captain who recognised the threat rats posed on a ship when it came to food and other supplies.

At this time more commonly known as Blackie, Simon was quick to make himself useful below decks and, barely more than a year old, like most young moggies took great pride in laying out his victims. Occasionally these gory trophies would be left in the seamen's bunks, and when he could get away with it Simon would sleep curled up in the captain's cap or risk pinching ice cubes out of the drinking water in the wardroom.

In the spring of 1949, now under the command of Lieutenant Commander Bernard M. Skinner, *Amethyst* was ordered up the Yangtze River to Nanking. Its mission was to replace the duty ship there, HMS *Consort*, which was serving as a guard ship for the British embassy during the civil war being fought between China's communist People's Liberation Army (PLA) and the Kuomintang Chinese Nationalists.

About a hundred miles upriver, on the morning of 20 April in what became known as the Yangtze Incident, the vessel came under sudden and very heavy fire from a PLA battery. This was the first time a Royal Navy crew had been ordered to action stations, with tin helmets on, since the war ended in 1945. The first shells fortunately passed harmlessly over *Amethyst*'s superstructure, but a subsequent volley tore through the bridge, fatally wounding the captain. Further shelling resulted in major damage to the port-side engine room and the sickbay. A badly injured officer was able to send one last, incomplete transmission – 'Under heavy fire. Am aground in approx position 31.10' North 119.50' East. Large number of casualties' – but immediately afterwards the generator was hit, leaving the stricken ship a helpless and immobile target.

Within the hour, and with 12 members of the ship's company dead, the remaining crew were ordered to abandon ship. Around 60 made it to safety on the opposite bank but several more were cut down in the water by PLA snipers. A further 52 remained on board, 12 of them seriously wounded, and all quickly found themselves unable to move around for fear of being picked off by communist riflemen on the bank.

In total the ship had taken more than 50 direct hits, and while efforts were being made to plug a number of holes below the waterline using bedding and anything else that came to hand, *Consort* was spotted bearing down on them. Steaming at full speed, and with her 4.5-inch guns blazing, she succeeded in taking out another enemy position but at a cost of another nine dead and three more injured.

Amethyst was eventually taken in tow and pulled beyond the range of the deadly shore battery, but further progress proved impossible. In the stalemate that followed, the stricken ship was unable to move for the next ten weeks. Braving fire from the ground, a Royal Air Force Sunderland flying boat was able to drop off a replacement medical officer – the ship's own MO was among the dead – but under the vigilant eye of the PLA and with no chance of replenishing its stores, the crew was immediately put on the tightest possible rations, their position clearly extremely hazardous

With 17 crew dead or dying, Simon too was among the

casualties and was found passed out in the wreckage with severe shrapnel wounds to his legs and back and burns to his face. He is assumed to have been kipping in the captain's cabin when a shell ripped a 15-foot hole through the adjacent bulkhead, and was caked in blood with his eyebrows and whiskers singed off.

Clearly patching up a cat was on no one's list of priorities, although with stores running desperately low – and the rats breeding fast in the hot humid atmosphere and being brave enough actually to bite the crew – Simon's hunting skills were needed more now than ever. Despite the severity of his injuries he rose magnificently to the challenge, and after taking very little time to recover – during which four pieces of shrapnel were pulled from his body, the healing process assisted by his determined licking – he was soon exceeding his normal peace-time tally of kills although it was noted that his whiskers had grown back bent.

After dispatching one large and particularly voracious specimen – nicknamed Mao Tse-tung following its repeated and costly raids on the ship's stores – Simon was promoted to able seaman in recognition of his tireless and invaluable service. At the same time he worked hard keeping up the crew's spirits. Joining the MO on ward rounds, Simon's friendly, purring demeanour proved to be a tonic for a number of traumatised and badly injured sailors.

On 30 July, with rations and fuel now at rock bottom and negotations with the Chinese deadlocked, it was decided to make a break for it at high water. Under cover of darkness the shell-scarred *Amethyst* slipped her moorings and limped down-river, taking hits much of the way. She was finally met toward the mouth of the river by HMS *Concord* and escorted back to Hong Kong at the end of an ordeal which had lasted 101 days.

After responding to an order from George VI in London for

the crew to splice the mainbrace, Able Seaman Simon was awarded the *Amethyst* campaign ribbon at the China Fleet Club. The following citation was read out:

> Able Seaman Simon, for distinguished and meritorious service on HMS *Amethyst*, you are hereby awarded the Distinguished Amethyst Campaign Ribbon.
>
> Be it known that on April 26, 1949, though recovering from wounds, when HMS *Amethyst* was standing by off Rose Bay, you did single-handedly and unarmed stalk down and destroy 'Mao Tse Tung', a rat guilty of raiding food supplies which were critically short.
>
> Be it further known that from April 22 to August 4 you did rid HMS *Amethyst* of pestilence and vermin, with unrelenting faithfulness.

With the crew's homecoming broadcast around the English-speaking world by the likes of Pathé news and Movietone, Simon and the sailors were greeted as heroes at each port of call from Singapore and Penang through the Suez Canal to Malta and Gibraltar. The ship's chances of escape had never been rated above 50:50, and the stoicism and courage shown by the crew clearly struck a note of optimism with a population still struggling to rebuild homes and lives after the war against Germany and Japan.

As for the ship's cat, no less stoical, he even made it into the American magazine *Time*, an edition of what has long been the biggest-selling weekly magazine, reporting how 'Simon got his white whiskers singed by a Communist shell, his face and legs scratched by shrapnel' but throughout the *Amethyst*'s cruise carried on in his billet and caught at least one mouse every day.

While the ship itself remained in Hong Kong undergoing

repairs, a committee of the Armed Forces Mascot Club met to consider a suggestion that this very special cat be recognised with the award of a Dickin Medal. Shortly afterwards the decision was taken unanimously to dispatch a collar ribbon to the crew of the *Amethyst*, the intention being to present the medal itself to Simon when the vessel returned home to Britain.

When the crew finally made it back they were met by Prime Minister Clement Attlee, and the date for Simon's presentation was set for 11 December 1949 in the presence of both Maria Dickin and the Lord Mayor of London. But sadly it was never to be. Required like any ordinary cat to spend several months in quarantine, Simon became listless a couple of weeks ahead of the ceremony and, sickening with a temperature and severe enteritis, he died quietly on the night of 27 November. He was still only a young cat but his injuries had left him unable to fight off a virus; it has been suggested that away from his ship and his friends Simon's spirit may simply have preferred to slip away to the sea.

When the news of his death broke, the quarantine centre in Surrey was inundated with letters, cards and flowers, and the distress of the crew was plain to see. Just as *Life* and other pictorials had reported Simon's homecoming so *Time* now noted his sad passing, and after being laid in a specially made casket draped in the Union flag, Simon – even now the only cat to win the Dickin Medal – was buried with full Naval honours in Plot 281 at the charity's animal cemetery at Ilford.

Presented posthumously shortly afterwards, Simon's Dickin Medal remained on HMS *Amethyst* until she was scrapped in 1957, and rightly so. After a period on consignment to the Naval Trophy Store at HMS *Nelson* in Portsmouth this unique and wonderful artefact was offered for auction in the 1960s, a move the Royal Navy might now regret as Simon's is to date

the only Dickin Medal presented to an animal on active duty
in the Senior Service. In 1993 it was sold again, securing a
winning bid of just a whisker under £23,500 – against an estimate of just £3,000 – with Simon subsequently being described
by the BBC as 'the most famous cat in British military history'.

Today there is a memorial plaque to Simon at the PDSA
PetAid hospital in Plymouth. A number of artefacts connected
with the ship's siege can still be seen aboard HMS *Belfast* in the
Thames, which like *Amethyst* was at that time part of the Royal
Navy's South China Sea Squadron. And sharp-eyed viewers of
the 1957 film *Yangtse Incident: The Story of HMS* Amethyst –
starring Richard Todd, William Hartnell and the real *Amethyst*,
which was brought out of mothballs – may also spot a black and
white cat in several scenes.

Chapter 2

Don't Shoot the Messenger

As we have seen, many of those members of the public unable to don a uniform but keen to contribute something meaningful to the Allied war effort in 1939–45 showed considerable imagination and ingenuity when it came to devising new ways to do it. By far the most widespread example of this was the estimated 250,000 homing and racing pigeons provided by fanciers up and down the country. Lent or given to assist with the formation of a new National Pigeon Service from 1939, fewer than 10 per cent of them were destined to come home at the end of the war.

Those generously volunteered by their owners included some prize-winning specimens from the royal lofts on the Sandringham estate in Norfolk. Others came from the paternalistic department store magnate Sir Ernest Debenham (the hen houses on whose Dorset estate were converted to provide accommodation for NPS birds) and from Lady Mary Manningham Buller, whose daughter went on to become the head of MI5. The majority, however, came from ordinary pigeon fanciers keen to do their bit, and their contribution was to be immense.

Such birds had already demonstrated their immense value in the field. As early as September 1914 the French had provided an example of what might be achieved by sending some 72 lofts to the front during the First Battle of the Marne. Similarly, as the continental war progressed in their favour, the Germans are thought to have commandeered as many as a million Belgian birds for the Kaiser's service. (Years later, in 1931, an edition of the *Illustrated London News* included a photograph taken in Berlin of a war memorial to the 'carrier pigeons of Germany' but said nothing about the leading Belgian pigeoneer who decided to kill 2,500 of his beloved birds rather than see them fall into enemy hands.)

Britain recognised that it needed something similar of its own, resulting in the formation of the Army Pigeon Service under Lieutenant (later Lieutenant Colonel) A. H. Osman. Such was its success that it was felt necessary under Regulation 21A of the 1914 Defence of the Realm Act to remind the public 'that homing pigeons are doing valuable work for the governement', and that 'killing, wounding or molesting homing pigeons is punishable by six months imprisonment or a £100 fine'. The same legislation permitted a £5 reward to be paid to anyone providing information leading to the conviction of an offender.

With a new war appearing on the horizon, it fell to Osman's son, Major W. H. Osman, to suggest in a letter to the Committee for Imperial Defence that a similar organisation be created once more. His letter was dated 11 November 1937, and with a sub-committee duly formed it was not to be long before the new National Pigeon Service went on to play an even more vital and decisive role.

The result of Major Osman's initiative was from the start a well-organised but still volunteer operation, the launch of which was announced in an edition of the journal *Flight* on 18 May 1938 calling for fanciers to make their birds available. Based in Gloucester, it was very soon able to provide a variety of Royal Air Force, army and special service units with trained and exceptionally fit birds. Capable of carrying messages over vast distances in very testing conditions and often at quite astonishing speeds, British pigeons were widely recognised as the finest racing birds anywhere and were freely given by fanciers despite the best of them and most cherished being worth as much as £5 a head – a substantial sum at the time.

Inevitably many of those much-prized birds were never seen again, but those who successfully battled through often quite appalling weather – not to mention the additional dangers of wartime – are now known to have saved many thousands of Allied and civilian lives. Often they did this by ensuring that vital intelligence was rapidly carried back through enemy lines to keep the War Office in London abreast of any and every significant development in continental Europe. Interestingly, consideration was also given to using other birds in slightly more sinister roles. In 1999, for example, the BBC reported that newly released MI5 documents revealed the existence of a crack wartime squad of peregrine falcons trained to spot and kill 'Nazi pigeons' bred by the Germans and sent across the Channel.

Another report, circulated immediately after the war by Wing Commander W. D. Lea Rayner, chief of the Air Ministry Pigeon Service, claimed his service was able to 'train pigeons to home to any object on the ground when air-released in the vicinity'. According to the highly capable Lea Rayner, 'bacteria might be delivered accurately to a target by this means [and] with the latest developments in explosives and bacterial science

I suggest that this possibility should be closely investigated and watched'.

Such plans were fortunately never to see the light of day, however, so that just as the threat of Heinrich Himmler's feathered Gestapo never quite materialised on these shores, the birds of the NPS – including many PDSA Dickin Medal winners among them – are today associated far more with lives saved than with the lives they might otherwise have threatened.

Beachcomber
Pigeon No. NPS 41. 4230
Date of Award: 6 March 1944
For bringing the first news to this country of the landing at Dieppe, under hazardous conditions in September 1942, while serving with the Canadian Army.

In the words of a former Canadian minister of state speaking to surviving veterans nearly 70 years later, the Allies' Dieppe Raid of 1942 was nothing less than a 'tragedy of epic proportions'. The bare facts, he told the gathering, were well known to everyone in the room: of the 5,000 of the minister's countrymen who embarked from England on the morning of 19 August, fewer than half returned unscathed. Behind them the retreating troops left 1,946 to sit out the next three years as prisoners of war and a staggering one thousand dead.

In fact, including other Allied troops and those involved in the naval and air cover which accompanied the assault on the German-occupied port, the total strength that day was just over 6,000, of whom 3,623 – nearly 60 per cent – were injured, killed or captured. In the retreat hundreds of weapons and vehicles were left on the beach; also lost were 106 aircraft (to just 49 Luftwaffe downed), more than 30 landing craft and one destroyer with a loss of a further 550 casualties. That said of course, and as with any action, the statistics, the numbers, no matter how appalling, scarcely tell the story. But by any standards Dieppe was a fiasco.

Even now the aims of what officially was termed Operation Jubilee are not at all clear, although it has been said repeatedly that much of the impetus for it came from the sometimes questionable personal ambition of the Chief of Combined Operations at the time. In the wake of the Dunkirk disaster, Vice Admiral Lord Louis Mountbatten may have simply intended it to be a morale booster, or wished to demonstrate – since there was no realistic hope of maintaining a hold on the heavily guarded port for long – that it was possible to capture such a stronghold temporarily and to glean useful intelligence from any captives before withdrawing.

Certainly the Germans had no idea what they were facing, and after capturing the Canadians' principal military landing officer demanded to know what he thought was going on. From their perspective it was too big for a raid and too small for an invasion, and the Canadian's reply has since gone down in history: 'If you can tell *me* the answer,' he told his interrogators, 'I would be very grateful.'

Hitler was naturally delighted at the outcome, calling it 'the first time the British have crossed the sea to offer the enemy a complete sample of their weapons', and whatever the objective, it is not hard to see why the operation failed. Firstly, as Mountbatten almost certainly planned the assault on the French coast without any specific external authorisation, it is likely that the troops on the ground were forced to engage the enemy without sufficient resources and the necessary military intelligence. Secondly they were required to mount a fairly unimaginative full-frontal assault on the Germans at a time when the latter were well armed and at a particularly high state of alert after being warned by French double agents that something was afoot.

As the shocking loss of ships, fighters and bombers suggest, the RAF was unsuccessful in its bid to negate German air cover in a battle it had initially expected to win by sheer force of numbers. When it came to putting men ashore the position was no better, tanks becoming bogged down or actually sinking while ferocious fire rained down on the infantry from guns concealed in the many caves which perforate the high cliffs in the area. (Once a retreat was ordered not a single tank made it back to England, and without exception their crews were killed or captured.)

Further evidence of the ferocity of the battle on the ground can be taken from the award of no fewer than three Victoria Crosses, an exceptional tally for any single action and particularly one which ended in failure. That two of the recipients immediately became prisoners of war speaks for itself. The courage shown by all the raiders was extraordinary, leaping into the bloodied waters and wading ashore knowing that once there they would have to scramble up the beach through an almost unimaginable hail of machine-gun fire. Fighting their way towards objectives which were themselves unclear, while all around friends and comrades fell, it became increasingly obvious that the mission was certain to fail.

The job of communicating the news of that failure fell to the Royal Canadian Corps of Signals, a body well known for its skill and tenacity when it came to laying many hundreds of miles of telephone and telegraph cables, often during the heat of battle. The corps was also responsible for all wireless sets and radios in the field, although on this occasion – and like so many of their Allied comrades over the next three years – they were to rely on a far older and arguably more sophisticated form of technology, namely the pigeon.

Although it had become clear early on in the day that the Germans knew the assault was coming, the planners of Operation Jubilee had insisted on maintaining total radio silence until their objectives – whatever they might have been – had been met. Because of this the first intelligence report of the disaster was sent back to England by pigeon, two of which were released at the earliest opportunity from a beachhead position.

The first was reportedly killed by German fire almost immediately, but the second – a bird bred in Ipswich and volunteered by an owner in Wolverton, Buckinghamshire – made it home. To Beachcomber's leg was attached a message addressed to the 1st Canadian Corps. In it Major General J. H. Roberts had written, 'Very heavy casualties in men and ships. Did everything possible to get men off but in order to get any home had to come to sad decision to abandon remainder. This was joint decision by Force Commanders. Obviously operation completely lacked surprise.'

While not the sole reason for the operation's failure, the lack of the element of surprise clearly contributed to the disaster at Dieppe and to the horrific toll of casualties. Mountbatten subsequently justified the raid, arguing that the lessons learned from it went towards ensuring the successful outcomes of Operation Torch in North Africa and the later D-Day landings by giving the Allies 'the priceless secret of victory'. For every man who died in Dieppe, he is reported to have said, 'at least ten more must have been spared in Normandy in 1944'.

There may be some truth to this, particularly when it came to designing new armoured assault vehicles and improving the RAF's ground support tactics for future operations. But aside from the terrible human cost Dieppe was a gift to Nazi propagandists as well as to Hitler personally, and in London strenuous efforts were made to discover how news of the raid had reached German ears.

Intriguingly, for a while, the finger of suspicion pointed to a compiler of the crossword in the *Daily Telegraph*, who 48 hours ahead of the operation had included 'French port' as a clue with 'Dieppe' as the answer. An investigation was ordered immediately led by Lord Tweedsmuir, son of the writer John Buchan and an officer attached to Canadian Military Intelligence. After an exhaustive inquiry his conclusion was that it was no more than 'a fluke', but for a short while the idea persisted that this most respectable broadsheet was being used to transmit vital secrets to enemy agents in the field.

Beachcomber, meanwhile, received his medal a little over a year and a half later, presented by Dorothea St Hill Bourne, secretary of the PDSA Allied Forces Mascot Club, and in June 2010 *Pigeon Service Message Book 418B*, used to record and distribute the first report of the raid's failure, went on display in the Canadian town of Dieppe, New Brunswick.

Gustav
Pigeon No. NPS 42. 31066
Date of Award: 1 September 1944
For delivering the first message from the Normandy Beaches from a ship off the beachhead while serving with the RAF on 6 June 1944.

One of the inspirations behind the 2005 animated film *Valiant*, in which a number of wartime messenger pigeons are voiced by Sir Ben Kingsley, Ricky Gervais and Ewan McGregor, Gustav accompanied many hundreds of birds released from the Normandy beaches during Operation Overlord, but was the first to make it back to England.

A grizzle cock, Gustav had been assigned to a war correspondent rather than a military unit, Montague Taylor of

Reuters, who had crossed the Channel with Allied forces while carrying with him a quartet of birds so that he could send dispatches back to the office via the Royal Air Force. Because of this the historic message attached to his leg seems even now to have a slightly more breathless newsy air to it than the usual military dispatches. Written very faintly in pencil, it reads, 'We are just twenty miles or so off the beaches. First assault troops landed 0750. Signal says no interference from enemy gunfire on beach . . . Steaming steadily in formation. Lightnings, Typhoons, Fortresses crossing since 0545. No enemy aircraft seen.'

Gustav, an English bird despite his somewhat middle-European moniker, was bred by a National Pigeon Service member from Cosham near Portsmouth. Thereafter he was trained by RAF Sergeant Harry Halsey a few miles away at Thorney Island, and over a period of two years flying messages out of occupied Belgium had built up a reputation as a fast and reliable flyer.

Naturally Overlord had been planned under conditions of the utmost secrecy, with Prime Minister Churchill leaving it until midday on 6 June to make his first public announcement to Parliament. The press were naturally frantic to hear more, however, and many journalists and photographers risked their lives to bring news back to their readers. In doing so they faced the same deadly fusillade of gunfire as the troops they accompanied onto the beaches, and to maintain radio silence relied on pigeons to transmit the news back home. Not all were fans of their feathered companions, however, and travelling with Taylor, Alan Melville of the BBC described them as 'cooing like mad things' and pecking him on several occasions. Nicknaming the four Blood, Sweat, Toil and Tears, he thought them 'wretched' but was happy to acknowledge their fitness for the job and in a later broadcast took back everything unkind that he had said.

With Taylor's dispatch coming from offshore, the first journalist actually to make landfall in France was Roger Greene of Associated Press. His first dispatch at 09.55 describes how he had

> landed at 0845, wading ashore waist-deep water under fire
> . . . Western part Atlantic Wall under tempestuous Allied
> assault. As I write, deeply dug in to beachhead, German
> prisoners, mostly wounded, streaming back but Boche still
> putting up terrific fight. Shells exploding all over beach and
> out at sea as wave after wave of Allied ships as far as eye
> can see sweeping into shore.

Getting even short reports such as this back to England was never less than highly problematic, and with details extremely sparse in the early stages the most the following morning's *Daily Telegraph* was able to carry was little more than an upbeat headline suggesting INVASION GOING WELL.

To circumvent the understandable requirement for radio silence some journalists leaned on returning officers to carry reports back to England by fast naval patrol vessel, but this was by no means reliable, and the very first dispatch from another Reuters man, Archibald Doon Campbell, who travelled with Lord Lovat's 1st Special Service commando brigade, promptly went astray. Other material reached England only to come to grief once it got there, including most famously that belonging to the celebrated Magnum photographer Robert Capa, whose film was accidentally ruined by a careless assistant.

Like the soldiers they accompanied, these reporters and cameramen evidently had to trust a lot to luck, assuming not just that they would overcome what Campbell in a surviving dispatch described as the 'bombs, shells, bullets and mines, to say nothing of booby traps [which], make each hour an age of grim experience', but also that some safe means could be found to get the message home. Pigeons offered the most obvious way to do this, although reports had to be kept concise and, as we have seen, their arrival was by no means guaranteed. Besides enemy marksmen and trained falcons along the coast, Gustav and his comrades faced the threat of stray bullets and other munitions and the everyday perils of long-distance flight. (The circumstances of his mission were officially recorded as adverse, but more descriptively by a senior RAF wing commander as 'a baddish day, when the weather was, um, British'.)

While Campbell famously sent his dispatch from 'a ditch 200 yards inside Normandy', the morning of 6 June found Taylor and Gustav on board an Allied landing ship tank (LST) with troops preparing for an amphibious assault. Released with the message capsule attached to one leg, after circling the reporter three times Gustav was required to travel some 150 miles back to his loft on Thorney Island. Despite a headwind estimated at approximately 30 mph and a sun obscured by heavy cloud, he completed the distance in five hours and 16 minutes, arriving back at his loft Sergeant Halsey was able to retrieve Taylor's dispatch, the first bringing news home of the operation to liberate continental Europe.

The success of Overlord doubtless explains in part the speed with which moves were made to recognise the bird and the action. On 27 November 1944 Gustav – together with another another bird, Paddy (see page 29) – was presented with a Dickin Medal by the wife of the First Sea Lord, Mrs Albert Alexander. For the benefit of a cameraman from Pathé News she lightly kissed both birds after placing the decorations around their necks.

Following the successful conclusion of the war, Gustav – or Sweat as Melville would have it – was returned home to his owner only to meet with disaster when the heroic bird was stepped on and killed by a member of the family cleaning out the loft. Having survived so much, Gustav's accidental death provides a melancholy coda to an otherwise fascinating footnote to D-Day history.

Gustav DM with Mrs A V Alexander, wife of the First Lord of the Admiralty with Wing Commander W Lea Raynor and Corporal Randall, 17 November 1944

Ruhr Express
Pigeon No. NPS 43. 29018
Date of Award: May 1945
For carrying an important message from the Ruhr Pocket in excellent time, while serving in the RAF in April 1945.

After two years' consistently good work in Air-sea Rescue and emergency intercommunication service this pigeon was dropped by parachute within the enemy lines more than 300 miles from base and brought very valuable information in the best time recorded in this operation. One of the best performances of its kind on record 13th April, 1945 Ruhr Pocket.

In April 1994 Dix Noonan Webb, a leading numismatist and military medals auction house based in Mayfair, offered an unusual and highly intriguing lot in its spring sale. Lot 327 comprised not just a Dickin Medal inscribed on the reverse 'N.P.S. 43.29018/ Ruhr Express/R.A.F./Ruhr/April 1945/AFMC 1052/No.22' but displayed alongside it in a glazed case was the actual medal recipient. Following his death the bird had been professionally mounted by Rowland Ward, the long-established Piccadilly taxidermy firm. Still wearing a National Pigeon Service numbered leg ring, the result was now offered together with a lifesize oil painting of the bird with two companions – Agnes and Per Ardua (see page 43) – signed by the artist Edward Henry Windred Snr.

The dark chequer cock's story had begun more than 50 years previously, in 1943 in Kent, where he was bred and hatched at RAF Detling. (This former Royal Naval Air Station about three miles north-east of Maidstone now serves as the county showground.) After being trained at Detling and assigned his own NPS number (the name came much later) the bird went on to perform 'two years' consistently good work' in air-sea rescue and general communications before being selected in April 1945 for a special operation behind enemy lines.

On the final day of the previous month General Dwight D. Eisenhower, as supreme commander of the Allied forces in Europe, had issued a proclamation to all German forces now defending their own borders, demanding they lay down their arms and surrender. On 1 April sections of the US First and Third Armies had managed to link up at Lippstadt, thereby trapping Field Marshal Walther von Model's Army Group B in what became known as the Ruhr Pocket. The field marshal might have surrendered, but Hitler, increasingly distracted and remote in his bunker from the reality of his troops on the ground, was still able to impose his authority through the SS and Gestapo and was determined that all Reich forces should fight to the last.

On 3 April American forces were thus charged with reducing the size of the pocket still further, beginning with an attack on the Germans by Lieutenant-General Raymond S. McLain's XIX Corps. Low on supplies, von Model nevertheless made two ferocious but abortive attempts to break out, but it soon became clear that the Germans were certain to sustain a defeat of enormous proportions. In order to avoid or at least to minimise the bloodshed that would result from a drawn-out action of this sort, the Allies were keen to use any and every means to bring about the swiftest possible conclusion. This included the use of carrier pigeons, and together with a number of other birds NPS 43. 29018 was removed from his loft and put into a circular carton suspended from a two-foot diameter silk parachute. Placed aboard an RAF aircraft on 11 April the birds were parachuted behind German lines, where – according to a story published after the war in the *British Pigeon Racing Gazette* – the cock subsequently named Ruhr Express narrowly avoided being cooked and eaten by a hungry Nazi stormtrooper. According to the story, the latter's avarice triumphed over his hunger and apparently persuaded by the standing offer of a 'lavish reward paid to those who surrendered British racing pigeons' the unnamed German soldier exchanged the bird, still alive, for a dated receipt from his local command headquarters.

By this stage the Germans were more than aware of their likely fate, and with thoughts of an orderly surrender uppermost a decision was taken to release the bird on 11 April with a message containing 'very valuable information . . . considered to have had a direct influence on the progress of the war at that critical time'. Ruhr Express was off, and two days later – having flown in excess of 300 miles – he returned to his loft in London on the roof of a building north of St James's Park which had been requisitioned by the War Office. The journey across the North Sea had been made in record time – 'the Fastest Ever Bird to Fly from Germany' according to the painter Windred – all the more remarkable as Ruhr Express had been released 'single up' rather than in the company of others, which for racing birds is very much the norm.

With the war in Europe soon won, the bird – now christened Ruhr Express, coincidentally the name of a celebrated Avro Lancaster bomber, the first of its type to be built in Canada – was recommended for an award by a selection committee including Wing Commander W. D. Lea Rayner, chief of the Air Ministry Pigeon Service. The recommendation was accepted, and following the award of a Dickin Medal the story of Ruhr Express quickly became better known, and the bird itself the subject of the aforementioned painting.

On 8 September 1945, together with Per Ardua, Ruhr Express was put up for auction with his medal at the PDSA show held in the grounds of the Royal Hospital, Chelsea. With the proceeds going to the RAF Benevolent Fund, his new-found celebrity, speed and endurance naturally excited interest in his breeding potential, leading to a hammer price of £420. The successful bidders were S. and D. Bishop of Weybridge, breeders of many record-breaking pigeons but none with quite the backstory to match that of Ruhr Express.

The price paid was well in excess of the previous record for such a bird (£225, which had stood since 1924), and in 1994 Ruhr Express made headlines once again when he real-ised £5,800 at auction. Unfortunately this time the buyer's name was not revealed, but intriguing rumours persist that Ruhr Express together with his medal and portrait were spirited off to Japan by members of a secretive pigeon-worshipping cult.

Tommy
Pigeon No. NURP 41. DHZ 56
Date of Award: February 1946

For delivering a valuable message from Holland to Lancashire under difficult conditions, while serving with the National Pigeon Service in July 1942.

For an example of serendipity in wartime communications there is little to beat the exploits of a pigeon bred and trained by William Brockbank of Dalton-in-Furness in what was then Lancashire.

While many birds were volunteered for the National Pigeon Service, those retained by their owners and breeders continued to be exercised and raced during the war years. One such bird, known as Tommy, disappeared while taking part in a 1942 race from Nantwich in Cheshire, apparently after being blown off course. Incredibly he made it as far as the Netherlands, which had been under Nazi control since being overrun in less than a week by German forces in May 1940. Tommy's good fortune was to be found by a local postman who had the sense to pass the bird on to a member of the Dutch resistance rather than – as almost certainly happened to many other birds – simply cooking him up.

The young resistance worker, Dick Drijver from Sandpoort in north Holland, already had experience of working with such birds having concealed two of his own in explicit contravention of a regulation imposed by the invading Germans. This required all homing pigeons to be killed and their identifying leg rings handed in, but Drijver kept back two of his own, Tijger and Amsterdammer, disguising what he had done by handing in their rings attached to a pair of dead birds. The surviving pair he used to deliver messages around the resistance network before he was himself forced to go into hiding when his activities aroused suspicion.

After being contacted by the postman, he quickly identified Tommy as a British specimen. Nursing the exhausted bird back to health before setting it free to fly home, Drijver attached a note to its leg in the hope that Tommy's owner would find it and know what to do. The note identified the location of a German munitions works near Amsterdam and requested the finder to see that a coded receipt for the bird was broadcast on the BBC's Dutch service. The bird was released on 18 August 1942, and despite being winged by a German shooter or a Dutch Nazi sympathiser Tommy wheeled round and set off for his home loft.

The journey of more than 400 miles was completed by Tommy the following day. Many years later William Brockbank's daughter Joyce Higgin described for readers of the *Manchester Evening News* how the bird had struggled home 'against all the odds'. Mystified but doubtless delighted by the discovery, Mr Brockbank had found Tommy, who by this time had been missing from his loft for several weeks. The canister on his leg was opened to reveal a tiny roll of paper, which was passed on to the police and eventually decoded by staff at the RAF.

It's not known what action followed the revelation about the ordnance factory, but the story of chance and endeavour made something of a star of Tommy, particularly once his name was added to the Dickin Medal roll of honour. The presentation itself took place in February 1946 at the Anglo-Netherlands Society – sometimes called the Dutch Club – in the presence of staff from the London embassy and Dick Drijver, who had been flown over to witness the event. Tommy's medal was presented by Major General Van Oorschot of the Dutch Intelligence Service, with the Air Ministry making a present to Mr Drijver of two replacement pigeons.

After that it was back to Lancashire, where according to his daughter Brockbank remained 'a modest man and said it was all a fuss about nothing'. He was happy to show the bird locally and at agricultural shows after the war used Tommy's celebrity status to raise funds for a playing field in Dalton

G.I. Joe
Pigeon No. USA 43. SC. 6390
Date of Award: August 1946
This bird is credited with making the most outstanding flight by a US Army Pigeon in World War II. Making the 20-mile flight from British 10th Army HQ, in the same number of minutes, it brought a message which arrived just in time to save the lives of at least 100 Allied soldiers from being bombed by their own planes.

Long lived and well travelled – hatched in Algiers, active in Tangiers, Bizerte and on the Italian front, and after his death in Detroit stuffed and mounted for display in New Jersey – G.I. Joe served with the United States Army Pigeon Service and is fondly recalled by his countrymen as the single most exceptional bird of the war.

The unusual award in August 1946 of a Dickin Medal to a foreign animal recognised not just his unstinting service but also the fact that by his most memorable flight G.I. Joe saved literally scores of British lives – as many as 1,000 according to General Mark Clark, the American Fifth Army Commander – before his well-earned retirement at Detroit's Zoological Gardens.

The story of this 'most outstanding military pigeon in history' was originally revealed by Otto Meyer, a former commander of the US Army Pigeon Service. He related how in October 1943 the British 56th (London) Infantry Division was scheduled to attack the strategically important village of Calvi Vecchia, about 25 miles north-west of Naples. On the morning of the 18th the US XII Air Support Command was ordered to bomb the village in order to 'to soften the entrance for the British Brigade'. But perhaps fearing precisely just such an attack was on its way the German force which had hitherto held the settlement retreated, leaving only a very small rearguard. Because of this British troops of the 169th Infanty Brigade were able to enter the village with very little resistance, occupying it ahead of schedule and leaving themselves open to a 'friendly' attack unless an urgent message could be got through to their allies cancelling the planned air raid.

Unfortunately all attempts to relay the message failed, by radio and other means, and the decision was made to send G.I. Joe in the hope that he would reach the airfield before the bombers took to the air. In the event the little bird managed to cover 20 miles in as many minutes, arriving (as Otto Meyer put it) 'just as our planes were warming up to take off'. Literally one minute's delay and it might have been a different and decidedly tragic story, one of defeat snatched from the jaws of victory and likely to have been accompanied by extremely heavy casualties – among the local population as well as the troops – from what today has become euphemistically known as friendly fire.

This close brush with tragedy, the quick turnaround in Allied fortunes and (it has to be said) the American authorities' knack for morale-boosting propaganda quickly combined to make a bird hitherto known simply as USA. 43. SC. 6390 – an otherwise ordinary-looking dark chequer pied white flight cock – something of a folk hero. Press photographs abound of the bird and his handlers.

Following the cessation of hostilities he was taken to the United States and housed in the Churchill Loft at the Signal Corps Pigeon Breeding and Training Center based at Fort Monmouth, New Jersey, this is effectively a hall of fame for the crème de la crème among the corps' more than 54,000 birds. His travels were not yet over, however. Following a recommendation to the Mascot Club that his exploits on the Allies' behalf be officially recognised, G.I. Joe – in no small part as a representative of the corps and the birds' 3,150 human comrades – was invited back to Europe for an investiture at the Tower of London.

In the US the award was apparently not entirely understood, and at least one Washington newspaper (under the headline HONOR YANK PIGEON) excitedly reported that their bird was the first animal ever to be honoured with a Dickin Medal. In fact more than three dozen such medals had been struck by this time, although this should in no way detract from G.I. Joe's achievement or its impact. Certainly the location and the assembled VIPs would have borne this out, with the much-decorated Constable of the Tower, Field Marshal Lord Chetwode, on hand to welcome the American delegation – which included Major General Clayton L. Bissel, US military and air attaché at the time – and a full complement of Yeoman Warders in their traditional Tudor garb.

After G.I. Joe's citation had been read out by the Tower's Resident Governor, Lieutenant Colonel E. H. Carkeet James, the ribbon of the Dickin Medal was slipped over the bird's neck by Major General Sir Charles Keightley. Now director of military training at the War Office, his command of V Corps in Italy would have ensured that he understood well the nature and results of the action at Calvi Vecchia.

Filmed by British Pathé for later broadcast on the news, the ceremony was as serious and sombre as any of its type, although the surviving film reveals a small hint of humour on the part of the news cameraman and his editor. Just briefly a cutaway is made from the uniformed VIPs and the respectful crowd of onlookers to a slightly disdainful tabby cat. This emerges from an anonymous doorway off Tower Green to see what all the fuss is about and then turns away.

As for the hero of the day, G.I. Joe was returned to America shortly afterwards and eventually found his way to the aforementioned zoo. He remained there until his death in 1961, at the very respectable age of 18, dying just three days ahead of the D-Day anniversary celebrations. Stuffed and mounted and returned to New Jersey, he was finally put on display at the Historical Center at Fort Monmouth, the US Army Communications and Electronics Museum.

Chapter 3

Record Breakers: Faster Than a Speeding Bullet

Although all such birds will instinctively home, the enduring popularity of pigeon racing relies to a great degree on the fact that some inevitably prove much faster than others. Of course even with the best birds other factors can and do intervene – the weather, most obviously. But even knowing from military logs that a particular bird's mission may have been accomplished with the assistance of a strong tailwind it is nevertheless interesting to note that some of the birds described here were able to cover immense distances at speeds which still impress nearly 70 years later.

Over short distances with no message capsule attached most racing birds will achieve something close to 60 miles per hour, although 40 is probably a more typical cruising speed. Even at that speed flying is strenuous, however, and on a long flight a bird can lose two or three ounces – a fifth of its body weight

– and for this reason younger birds, which is to say one to four years old, show a better rate of recovery and tend to be preferred.

Younger birds are easier to train too, a process which typically takes around eight weeks from the time the bird is hatched. To begin with a timetable of short flights enables the bird to get its aerial bearings. By the end of the eighth week most should have the strength and stamina to fly for an hour and maybe 50 or 60 miles. Occasionally trainers will turn to tricks, such as using food as a motivator or even sex – a cock bird will be shown his mate with another male immediately before being sent on a mission.

With good reason many of the fastest birds of the war are still revered in racing circles, although the vast majority have never received the wider recognition which in retrospect they deserve. In May 1942, for example, a pied hen known only as NURP 40. PPC 488 travelled 86 miles in just 82 minutes, but as it was only on an air-release test flight from RAF Mount Batten, a flying-boat base in Devon, the bird's astonishing feat was merely noted down in the station's log.

At the time the convention was to record a bird's speed in yards per minute, although this particular flight equates to something in excess of 92 feet *per second*, a feat which is hard to visualise but which led, exactly a year later, to the same bird being selected to transmit an important message from the Chancellor of the Exchequer to the mayor of Plymouth concerning the Wings for Victory appeal, an initiative to encourage civilians to save money in government bonds rather than bank accounts. She also successfully completed some 50 operational sorties with a number of different flying-boat crews, yet today poor old NURP 40. PPC 488 is not even known by name.

Happily a few record breakers have achieved that recognition, although in at least one case, that of Per Ardua, the bird's near mythic status among international pigeon fanciers is in spite of her most glorious flight being completely accidental and definitely never authorised.

Taking her name from the motto of the Royal Air Force (*Per Ardua ad Astra* – Through Adversity to the Stars) this young red chequer hen was one of several pigeons transferred to Gibraltar in early November 1944. Somehow she escaped her loft while being rested before being sent on assignment, and without anyone noticing she had set off for home, which was well over 1,000 miles away. It took until 4 December for her absence finally to be noted, and on the 9th – weather-beaten and completely exhausted – she reappeared (as unexpectedly as she had disappeared) back at her home loft in Gillingham, Kent.

It is impossible to time the flight exactly, but at worst Per Ardua's journey up through Spain and France had taken her 12 days to cover an incredible 1,090 miles. The previous record for a racing bird was 1,001 miles in 28 days, and that was in peacetime. But even so, having gone AWOL, Per Ardua was sadly ruled ineligible for a conventional award and had to wait until after the war to make amends. Her chance came in September 1946, at an Allied Forces Mascot Club auction. With excited breeders and trainers bidding against each other, her sale raised £360 for the RAF Benevolent Fund charity, an astonishing price for the time and one which was to remain unbeaten by all except Ruhr Express on the same day (see page 33).

A few of the fastest birds have perhaps been more fortunate, and, managing to pull out all the stops when it really matters, a handful – admittedly one of them only posthumously – have received the recognition their achievements warranted.

Paddy
Pigeon No. NPS 43. 9451
Date of Award: 1 September 1944
For the best recorded time with a message from the Normandy Operations, while serving with the RAF in June, 1944.

In September 2009 the BBC reported that 'one of World War II's smallest war heroes' was to be honoured with a fly-past. The hero of the day was Paddy, a messenger pigeon who took part in the D-Day landings while on secondment from the Royal Air Force to the US First Army. The fly-past in his honour was performed by a flock of pigeons released over a new memorial to this very singular bird close to his former home in Northern Ireland.

Introduced to the press after his record-breaking flight as 'an Irish pigeon trained in England by a Scotsman with a Welsh assistant', Paddy was hatched and raised by Captain Andrew Hughes in Carnlough, County Antrim some 70 years ago. Before being sent with many thousands of other birds to RAF Hurn in Hampshire (now Bournemouth Airport) he was given the number NPS 43. 9451 and assigned to the air-sea rescue unit at RAF Ballykelly. Paddy soon attracted the attention of the authorities, being described by one handler as of 'exceptional intelligence', and he notched up the third-best performance among a loft of 80 birds. This led to him being attached to the US military, which intended using a number of British-trained birds for missions during the crucial D-Day landings.

The yearling cock was to be part of a mission (code-named U2) which involved the release of a total of 30 birds required to fly back from Normandy to Hurn. Braving poor weather conditions, all the usual dangers of conflict and even the threat of German-trained falcons deployed along the coast from Calais to intercept Allied carrier pigeons, the birds were nevertheless considered more secure than radio communications, which could fatally compromise military safety if intercepted.

It seems incredible now that getting news of such a momentous event relied on such a low-tech solution, but as one member of the RAF Beach Squadron HQ put it at the time, the operation was so critical to the outcome of the war that it was necessary for the invading force to think of everything. This, he said, included 'carrier pigeons to carry the big news home if all else fails [and] a wing commander arrived here only a few hours before I embarked on my landing ship tank to present me with a basket of four pigeons, complete with food and message-carrying equipment'.

According to the late John McMullan, a veteran pigeon fancier who helped Captain Hughes train many of his birds back in Ireland, Paddy was 'the last pigeon to be let go by the Americans in Normandy and he was the first one home. He was the best of the lot, the best of thousands.' Crucially his message was also the first to indicate the probable success of Operation Overlord, rather than merely commenting on its progress as other bird messages had done earlier on in the assault. Paddy was also one of an astonishing 46,532 birds supplied to US forces by British fanciers at this time.

History would seem to bear out McMullan's glowing description, with Paddy beating many hundreds of similar birds back to England and doing so by a margin of nearly half an hour. Released at 08.15 on 12 June Paddy's performance was by any standards impressive, and perhaps doubly so since on leaving Northern Ireland the bird had had to be retrained to recognise the RAF base as his new home. In the event he was able to cover 230 miles in just 4 hours 50 minutes – an average speed not far shy of 50 mph – arriving in his loft near Bournemouth with valuable intelligence about the Allies' progress in the long-awaited invasion of the German Reich.

A year later, after being demobbed, Paddy was returned to Carnlough and Captain Hughes, who looked after him until the bird's death in 1954. Something of an unlikely local hero, but deservedly so as the only Irish PDSA Dickin Medal recipient, Paddy's legend was to live on. In 1999 a former Irish Army commandant paid almost £7,000 for the medal when it was auctioned in Dublin, and in 2003 Paddy himself became the star of an illustrated children's book, *Paddy the Pigeon* written by Gail Seekamp.

In 2009, however, the need was felt locally for a more public and permanent memorial to the town's little wartime hero, and the Larne and District Historical Society decided to put a plaque on the harbour wall at Carnlough describing Paddy's exploits.

The occasion of its unveiling was marked by the release at the town's Carnegie Museum and Art Centre of a number of pigeons which duly performed the aforementioned feathered fly-past. The society asked 88-year-old John McMullan to perform the unveiling, and naturally keen to see his special bird recognised in this way he was happy to oblige. On the day he was able also to add to the legend, revealing that during his initial training Paddy had been taken out into the Irish Sea by submarine to see whether he could find his way home – which of course, with ease, he could. John McMullan sadly died a few short weeks later.

Paddy

William of Orange
Pigeon No. NPS 42. 15125
Date of Award: May 1945
For delivering a message from the Arnhem Airborne Operation in record time for any single pigeon, while serving with the APS in September 1944.

The subject of the star-studded epic *A Bridge Too Far*, the assault on Arnhem is one of the better-known operations from the closing stages of World War II. Today it is often recalled as the last great failure of the British Army, but as the principal British field commander General Sir Bernard Montgomery was quick to note as the dust settled, 'in years to come it will be a great thing for a man to be able to say: I fought at Arnhem'.

While wholly unsuccessful in its key objective – to force an entry into Germany across the Rhine in order to bring an earlier close to the war – Operation Market Garden, in 1944 the largest airborne assault ever attempted, is considered by many historians to have set the standard for the Parachute Regiment. For the general public too it remains a proud byword for the indefatigable spirit of the British fighting man. That said, and although the fighting north of the Rhine still stands as a fine example of courage and endurance on the part of soldiers on the ground, it was a disaster for thousands of them and for the British 1st Airborne Division one from which it never recovered.

On its return to England this was shattered beyond recognition, having lost three-quarters of its strength including three brigade commanders, eight out of nine battalion commanders and more than four-fifths of its infantry company commanders. In all, Allied airborne units lost 1,485 killed or wounded during what became known as the Battle of Arnhem with more than 6,500 listed as captured or missing.

Fewer than 4,000 made it home, and with many hundreds more forced into hiding in Holland, the authorities in London – much like Montgomery – were quick to acknowledge the soldiers' bravery and fortitude in the face of implacable odds. With an investiture ceremony hastily organised at Buckingham Palace, a list was published of 59 servicemen who were to be decorated – an unprecedented five of whom to be awarded the Victoria Cross.

Regardless of its eventual outcome, any military operation, more so such a large one as Market Garden, relies on fast and accurate communication. Once again the hopes of Allied forces were pinned as much on their feathered comrades as on more advanced technologies, and while with the benefit of hindsight poor communication cannot be divorced from the exceptionally heavy losses, one such bird – William of Orange – more than excelled himself on the day.

This regally named mealy cock was bred by Sir William Proctor Smith, the prominent Cheshire landowner who originated the Sion strain of racing birds which is still so beloved of modern fanciers. Offered by his owner to the Army Pigeon Service, after training William of Orange was assigned to the Royal Corps of Signals. The bird proved itself exceptionally fast, on one occasion completing a 68-mile training flight in 58 minutes, an achievement which would have required him to maintain an average speed in excess of 2,000 yards a minute.

Once these abilities were recognised, William of Orange was selected for special duties, possibly as part of MI14, a now-defunct department of the British Directorate of Military Intelligence which was charged with collecting intelligence about the German homeland and frequently used such birds.

It was from confidential documents relating to MI14 and released in 2004 that the public first learned of some of the more bizarre pigeon initiatives which were considered. These included one where 'a thousand pigeons each with a two-ounce explosive capsule, landed at intervals on a specific target, might be a seriously inconvenient surprise'. But although MI6 reportedly liked the idea of spreading chaos in this way, MI5 dismissed the scheme's promoter as 'a menace', and most of the birds assigned to MI14 accordingly found themselves dropped behind enemy lines equipped with little more than a message canister.

William of Orange was to accompany the more than 34,000 men of the 1st Airborne, the US 101st and 82nd Airborne Divisions, and the Polish Brigade being deployed to the area around Arnhem by glider and parachute on 17 September. The assault required an extraordinary flotilla of aircraft to be assembled, including more than 1,400 transport planes, 321 converted bombers and nearly 3,200 British and American gliders, many of them without a co-pilot as insufficient numbers of these could be found.

Unfortunately communication by wireless ran into problems almost immediately, in part because the equipment carried by the forward troops lacked the necessary range to link the area of the assault with the divisional HQ. Instead contact with England relied on the pigeons dropped with the troops, and on 19 September, at around 10.30, William of Orange was released over the battlefield with an important dispatch. Getting home required a high-speed dash of some 260 miles – 135 of them over open water – and the bird reached his home loft a mere four hours and 25 minutes later.

Under any circumstances this would have been an impressive achievement, and on a day when the weather conditions in both Arnhem and England were far from favourable it was nothing short of remarkable. Managing to average 1,740 yards a minute against a background of weather bad enough to halt all other airborne operations, William of Orange's historic flight is thought never to have been equalled.

With the weather closing in and communication on the ground further hampered by the wooded terrain, the Allies' front-line troops nevertheless lacked the air support they so badly needed. Soon outflanked and running low on ammunition, physical exhaustion and hunger also took their toll and to most it must have been obvious that the operation was going to end in failure.

From the start it had probably been doomed, the Allies believing German defences in the area were relatively poor when in fact two divisions of I SS Panzer Corps were in the area and had even been practising in recent weeks how to tackle an Allied airborne attack. The Americans enjoyed some success, but British troops had landed too far from their objective thereby losing the element of surprise.

By the 25th it was all over, and Montgomery ordered those of his men who could do so to withdraw. Like William of Orange they had done their best, but on this occasion the odds had been too heavily stacked in the enemy's favour. Happily William survived the war, and returned to Cheshire. Some ten years later he was reported by Sir William still to be in fine shape, and his name is well known among fanciers as the father (and grandfather) of a number of championship-winning birds. Following his death, and that of Sir William, in 1965 Lady Smith presented the medal to the Royal Signals Museum at Blandford Camp in Dorset.

Unnamed
Pigeon No. DD 43. T 139
Australian Army Signal Corps
Date of award: February 1947
Carrying a message through a severe tropical storm thereby bringing help to an Army boat with vital cargo, in danger of

foundering. While serving with Australian Corps of Signals in south-west Pacific in June, 1945.

One of two Australian birds to be awarded the Dickin Medal (see page 90), Army Pigeon DD 43. T139 was deployed to the area around the Huon Gulf in 1944, an important coastal region of what is now Papua New Guinea. Stretching more than 100 miles from Cape Cretin in the north-east to Cape Ward Hunt, the gulf's 170-mile shoreline saw some exceptionally fierce fighting during the see-saw campaign between American and Australian allies and an island-hopping Japanese invasion force.

At the outbreak of the war this large and strategically important island in the south-west Pacific was still divided into two halves, with administrative control split between Australia and the Netherlands. As early as 1942, keen to extend their territory, the Japanese had made their first amphibious landings in the Huon Gulf, but were driven off during the Battle of the Coral Sea before they could achieve their objective of Port Moresby. After their massive defeat at the hands of the Americans at Midway, however, a fresh attempt was made with the Japanese this time reaching Moresby before being driven back again to Kokoda by a successful counter-offensive. This was led by General Thomas Blarney, who had recently taken command of the Australian Army.

As the conflict continued, the fighting took place mostly in the highlands and northern and eastern parts of the island, many local Papuans giving vital assistance to their colonial overlords by carrying equipment and injured men and at times fighting alongside Australian troops. But despite many Allied successes the Japanese chose to fight on and, ignoring their truly horrific casualty figures, the vast majority refused to surrender until September 1945 when the war came to an end.

In March 1943, for example, a typically brutal encounter saw a Japanese convoy steam across the gulf carrying nearly 6,400 heavily armed troops. Coming under sustained attack from relays of Australian and US aircraft – more than 250 in total – the 5,000-ton *Kyokusei Maru* and the 3,800-ton *Shinai Maru* were quickly sunk together with four of the Japanese destroyers sent to accompany the convoy.

The death toll was immense, with as many as 3,000 Japanese soldiers and crew men being lost in very short order. Many of these died from shark attacks after their lifeboats and rafts were hit and sunk by Allied fighters. These had been ordered to attack by commanders determined to prevent Japanese military personnel making it to the shore to reinforce their comrades, who were well dug in. The Japanese also lost 63 aircraft, to a loss of just three Allied fighters and two bombers, in what rapidly turned into a bloody turkey shoot.

To the north, in the area around the port at Madang, the fighting was perhaps fiercer still, and indeed 70 years later the area has become popular among recreational divers who visit Papua New Guinea expressly to explore the more than 30 American and Imperial Japanese wrecks – naval and air – which litter the seabed of Hansa Bay. In 1942 the Japanese had managed to capture the town of Madang more or less unopposed, but by September of that year a ferocious counter-attack was under way involving both US and Australian forces determined to wrest contol of the harbour and two airfields from the invaders.

The counter-attack involved sustained air assault and naval bombardment, and continued throughout 1943 with the Japanese refusing to yield. By now well dug in, they were able to call on one of the largest ammunition dumps in the Pacific, and it was well into 1944 before the Australians managed to retake the badly shattered town. What had been a very useful supply base for the Japanese as they made their way across the Pacific, Madang now became a decisive hub for the Allies and remained a busy centre for military shipping until the very conclusion of the war.

In such an environment pigeons were to prove invaluable, the wild and rugged terrain posing special problems not just by increasing the chances of conventional communication lines being cut but because even the heaviest, most durable wireless sets could fail in the extreme humidity of the jungle. Far more portable and easy to feed and water, a pair of pigeons could operate efficiently and silently – and if the enemy did take a potshot at one of them he would do so at the risk of exposing his position. Once harnesses replaced leg canisters, pigeons could carry maps showing the position of enemy patrols (or reefs where a landing force might hit trouble) and for servicemen in trouble they could also provide a crucial lifeline when communication with HQ was critical.

In July 1945, with Hitler dead and the Japanese empire entering its last few desperate weeks as a military power, the Allied Water Transport Group Headquarters at Madang received a distress message from a craft foundering off the coast. The bird which carried the message, Army Pigeon No. DD 43. T139, was a blue bar cock which had already completed 23 operational flights totalling 1,004 miles on this occasion. It appears to have covered 40 miles through an exceptionally torrential tropical storm in just 50 minutes.

The message was brief but comprehensive, advising HQ that Army Boat 1402 was in dire straits: 'To: Detachment 55 Australian Port Craft Company, MADANG. From: A.B. 1402.

Date: 12.7.45. Engine Failed. Wash on to beach at WADAU owing very heavy seas. Send help immediately. Am rapidly filling with sand. TOO: 0800 – Senders signature – HOLLAND Cpl. TO Liberation 0805 – No. of copies 2. TOR at Loft – 0855'. A rescue attempt was launched immediately, which managed to locate the craft in time to rescue both its crew and a valuable cargo of arms, munitions and other equipment before the boat was wrecked on a small offshore island.

The flight was to be the bird's best in a relatively lengthy service life, T139 having been presented to the Australian Corps of Signals back in 1943 at the behest of George Adams of Footscray, Victoria. Interestingly, and despite being described as such on the certificate awarded to him by the Allied Forces Mascot Club, Adams was not himself a breeder. Instead, driven by the patriotic urge to contribute something meaningful to the Australian war effort, he had approached a number of racing clubs around the city of Melbourne to drum up support for the army's pigeons. At the Yarraville Racing Pigeon Club he was fortunate enough to fall in with breeder Gordon Whittle, who agreed to donate a few of his birds to Adams for this express purpose, the first batch including T139.

Coming as it did so close to the news of the final Japanese surrender, it is possible that the bird's flight somehow escaped the notice of the authorities in London. Certainly it was not until the summer of 1947 that the decision was taken to award T139 a Dickin Medal, and even then the citation described the rescue as having taken place a month earlier than actually it had. As an award to a foreign animal it is nevertheless particularly precious, and happily both it and the accompanying certificate now form part of the official Australian War Memorial, together with a signed photograph of the bird given by George Adams to Gordon Whittle.

Duke of Normandy
Pigeon No. NURP 41. SBC 219
Date of Award: 8 January 1947
For being the first bird to arrive with a message from Paratroops of 21st Army Group behind enemy lines on D-Day 6 June, 1944, while serving with APS.

Despite being the last surviving fragment of the White City complex which hosted the great Franco-British Exhibition of 1908 (not to mention London's first Olympic Games later on the same year) Frithville Gardens in Shepherd's Bush looks like the nondescript, ordinary inner-city street that it is. It lacks a blue plaque, as no one famous ever lived there; and these days one suspects that even most locals will not know much about its past although more than 8,000,000 visitors trooped through the 1908 exhibition before it finally closed. Nor, perhaps, have they heard of the street's decorated war hero, Duke of Normandy, despite this cock bird's name being well known among Britain's many thousands of pigeon fanciers.

The bird was bred by a naturalised Belgian living and working in Frithville Gardens, Gaston Noterman, a master organ builder and restorer from a family that had settled in this country some time before World War I. Many Noterman organs survive in and around London, and in pigeon circles the name Noterman is still associated with a number of successful birds racing at national and international level.

After being volunteered by his owner, NURP 41. SBC 219 was assigned to the Army Pigeon Service for training. On 6 June 1944, D-Day, the bird was dropped behind German lines with paratroopers of Montgomery's Anglo-Canadian Twenty-First Army Group and released after six days' close confinement in his basket. Despite bad weather on the morning of his release,

55

gales in the English Channel and exceptionally heavy rain, Duke of Normandy made it back to his loft in 26 hours and 50 minutes.

Unnamed
Pigeon No. NURP 43. CC 1418
Date of Award: 8 January 1947 (posthumous)
For the fastest flight with message from 6th Airborne Div. Normandy, 7 June, 1944, while serving with APS.

Under any circumstances the Duke's flight would have been an impressive performance, and indeed it was to be beaten by only one other bird taking part in the D-Day Landings. The bird in question, another unnamed hero, hen No. NURP 43 CC 1418, covered a very similar distance in just 23 hours and 4 minutes. As the only bird ever to home from this major airborne assault in under 24 hours she too became a Dickin Medal recipient, but only sadly only posthumously. She disappeared on a subsequent flight back from France, and her name – if indeed she was ever known by one – is also now lost.

Chapter 4

The Bomb Squad

Over many years sniffer or detection dogs have been used to alert handlers to the presence of a wide range of different things, ranging from endangered or invasive species (such as bumble bees and quagga mussels) to mobile telephones concealed by prison inmates and of course illegal drugs and explosives. As with search and rescue it is something for which the canine species are spectacularly well equipped and adapted, able as they are to differentiate between many different scents and in particular to locate the required one even in cases where efforts have been made to mask the scent or otherwise mislead the animal.

Specially trained dogs have managed, for example, to detect the tiniest traces of blood in a room, even after strenuous attempts have been made to clean up the scene of a crime. In a similar vein, in 2002 Australian newspapers ran stories about a sniffer dog in Queensland who had managed to identify a woman prison visitor as carrying marijuana even though she had concealed the drug in a balloon tucked into her bra having previously rubbed the contraband with a mixture of coffee, pepper and Vick's VapoRub.

Among the most demanding tasks for such animals, however, are those involving mine detection and clearance with their combination of environmental challenges and extreme hazard. It is a task they have been called upon to do since World War II, and which they have continued to do more recently in Iraq and Afghanistan. This is despite some initially poor results which followed from a number of dogs becoming simply too stressed to remain inside the combat zone.

Once again many of the dogs that showed the earliest promise in this regard were volunteers, much-loved animals donated by owners keen to do their bit or 'be involved somehow or other', or who felt they could no longer feed them adequately once rationing began to bite in the 1940s. For a while it was an offence to give an animal any food that was suitable for human consumption, and at a time when pets were also not allowed in air-raid shelters (by early 1940 in London alone 400,000 of them had been put down by the RSPCA) owners may simply have thought the military would be better able to take care of them. This was an understandable sentiment, if somewhat ironic given where many of them ended up.

Ricky
Welsh collie
Date of Award: 29 March 1947

This dog was engaged in clearing the verges of the canal bank at Nederweert, Holland. He found all the mines but during the operation one of them exploded. Ricky was wounded in the head but remained calm and kept at work. Had he become excited he would have been a danger to the rest of the section working nearby.

A graduate of the increasingly successful War Dogs Training School based at Northaw in Hertfordshire in premises commandeered from the Greyhound Racing Assocation, Ricky was volunteered for war service in 1944 by his owner. Mrs Litchfield of Bromley in Kent had bought the shaggy long-haired sheepdog puppy for seven shillings and sixpence earlier in the year and reportedly made it clear that the dog was merely on loan. On leaving the school Ricky was assigned to 279th Field Company of the 15th (Scottish) Infantry Division and put into the care of Maurice Yelding, who had been a circus artiste before being called up.

The division had seen heavy action during World War I and had spent the entire duration on the Western Front, fighting in the Battle of Loos, the Somme Offensive of 1916 (including Pozières and Flers-Courcelette) and the 3rd Battle of Ypres. By the 1940s it had been recast as a second-line Territorial Army division, engaged in Normandy as part of the D-Day Landings and then three weeks later in Operations Epsom and Goodwood, which were bids to outflank and capture strategically important positions in and around the German-held town of Caen.

Thereafter the division was to play a supporting role in Operation Market Garden, the largely unsuccessful Allied assault on Germany and the Netherlands, and ended the war by advancing from the Rhine to the Baltic Sea. Enjoying the unique distinction of having led the final river crossing of the European war, across the Elbe on 29 April 1945, survivors today can also claim membership of the only British army division to have been involved in three of the six major European river assault crossings: Seine, Rhine and Elbe.

Ahead of this, however, early December 1944 found Ricky and Private Yelding in the Netherlands, engaged in the dangerous and essential task of mine detection and clearance. Since July of that year four platoons of sappers had been posted to north-west Europe, their sniffer dogs working seven days a week on mine clearance along literally hundreds of miles of roads, water- and railways. Ricky was set to work along the banks of the Noordevaart in the south-east. A canal in the municipality of Nederweert, this important waterway had initially formed part of an ambitious Napoleonic plan for the Grand Canal du Nord from the Rhine to the North Sea. In the nineteenth century it had been extended to assist with peat exports from the area, and had more recently seen fierce fighting in the struggle to drive the Germans back towards Berlin.

Although the work was hazardous the pair made a good team. 'He turned up as cheeky as ever,' Yelding had written in a letter from Northaw to Mrs Litchfield, 'and was instantly a favourite with the kennel girls. Luckily he is the unspoilable type and settled down to work.' When selected for overseas work, Yelding claimed to have had no hesitation in picking Ricky to go with him – 'a decision I have never regretted'.

Ricky was good at his work, locating mines concealed beneath deep gravel, in the undergrowth and even in the thickest of Dutch mud. What Yelding was later to describe as 'the nearest escape' the pair had took place on a freezing day in Holland while the two of them were working in tandem. The details of what happened were relayed to Mrs Litchfield by way of an extended quotation from an official dispatch concerning the operation.

'The above mentioned dog on the 3rd December 1944 was engaged in the task of clearing the verges of the canal bank at Nederweent [sic] Holland.' This was vital work, the Germans by this time employing 16 different types of anti-tank mine, 10 different types of anti-personnel mine and many different types of booby traps as they fought a largely defensive campaign which relied heavily on weapons of attrition. Against this background the dog, 'found all the mines and during the operation the Section Commander was blown up. Ricky was wounded in the head but kept on working and remained calm and collected. Had he become excited he would have been a danger to the rest of the Section who were working nearby.'

Yelding confirmed this description of events in his letter to Mrs Litchfield, cheerfully telling her that the events described were 'no exaggeration. You notice it says "nearby". We were actually within three feet of the mine and in the middle of a minefield. I am confident that [Ricky] was as steady as the Rock of Gibraltar and I think it was his coolness that brought us out of a sticky patch safely.'

Ricky continued working alongside his comrades until the end of the war and might have stayed on had the authorities' offer to buy him from Mrs Litchfield been accepted. According to Dorothea St Hill Bourne, secretary of the Allied Forces Mascot Club at the time, an offer was made of 'the maximum amount allowed for a dog' – the army being keen to retain a dog with such a record of steadfastness – but his owner was not to be persuaded, and she responded with a reminder of the original terms of the loan. Instead it was arranged for Ricky to travel home to Kent, Yelding in the meantime writing to assure Mrs Litchfield that 'I have still got him and as long as I am here I will look after him. I owe him that.' Nothing, he said, would make him happier than to see the dog he called Rag-Bag safely on the boat home and rejoining his family.

Firmly convinced of the value of such dogs, and finding it impossible to assess how many lives have been saved by them, Mrs St Hill Bourne was struck by the testimony of 'many men serving in France, Holland, Belgium and Germany' describing the enthusiasm the dogs showed for their work 'amid scenes of indescribable desolation'. An idea of the scale of the problem can also be gleaned from the startling fact that even now, in 2012, minefield clearance is still under way in the Netherlands and part of northern France.

Given this it was perhaps unsurprising that a request to the club for Ricky's service to be acknowledged was well received. In late 1946 he was recommended for the PDSA Dickin Medal, and in March the following year one was duly presented to the brave dog who had cost his owner the equivalent of just 37.5p.

Buster
Springer spaniel
Royal Army Veterinary Corps arms and explosives search dog
Date of Award: 9 December 2003
For outstanding gallantry in March 2003 while assigned to the Duke of Wellington's Regiment in Safwan, Southern Iraq. Arms and explosives search dog Buster located an arsenal of weapons and explosives hidden behind a false wall in a property linked with an extremist group. Buster is considered responsible for saving the lives of service personnel and civilians. Following the find, all attacks ceased and shortly afterwards troops replaced their steel helmets with berets.

Buster received his Dickin Medal from HRH Princess Alexandra, PDSA patron, at a special ceremony held at the Imperial War Museum in London exactly 60 years after the first such medal had been awarded. The five-year-old, an unwanted gun dog found in a rescue home, was credited with saving a number of lives during his service both during the Iraq War and afterwards when the struggle continued against insurgents in the south of that country.

The particular action referenced in Buster's medal citation that day had taken place seven months earlier in the town of Safwan on the Kuwaiti border. It followed an early-morning raid on what was thought to be a Ba'athist stronghold by approximately 200 Nato troops. When the objective had been secured as many as 16 supporters of Saddam Hussein were arrested, but nothing was found in the way of weapons or explosives. The Iraqis continued to insist that they had nothing to hide, but Buster and his handler, RAVC Sergeant Danny Morgan, then aged 37, were detailed to have a closer look around.

In such circumstances it is standard practice to allow the dog to enter a suspect building first in case the area is booby-trapped. Buster went in and, according to Sergeant Morgan, immediately 'became excited in a particular area, and I knew he'd discovered something'. In fact the dog had stumbled upon a cache of weapons, carefully concealed in a cavity in the wall behind sheet metal hidden by a wardrobe placed in front of it. The stash included AK-47 assault rifles, a pistol, several grenades, a quantity of ammunition and what looked like bomb-making equipment. At the same time the troops uncovered bags of money, some suspect drugs and literature apparently relating to the pro-Saddam Ba'ath Party.

While understandably very proud of the dog's abilities and his record, Sergeant Morgan later admitted to the press that to Buster this sort of thing is largely all a game. In an interview with the *Sun* newspaper he said that Buster's training involved 'teaching him to fetch weapons like guns and ammunition instead of sticks and balls. He loves his job simply because he thinks it's a game and obviously has no idea he's going into dangerous situations.' Nevertheless, says Morgan, Buster off duty has proved a great friend and family pet back home in Aldershot, Hampshire, while as 'the only arms and explosives search dog working in Iraq' he was 'worth his weight in gold'.

Lieutenant Colonel Gerald Dineley of the Army Medical Directorate was even more emphatic about the dog's performance in Safwan. 'Quite simply,' he said when the medal award was first announced, 'Buster succeeded where humans failed. A manual search of the building had failed to unearth any materiel and Buster was released into the house to continue the search. Within minutes . . . we found, concealed behind a purpose-built wall cavity, a stash of guns, grenades, ammunition, bomb-making equipment, explosive devices, drugs and propaganda material.'

As a result of the removal from use of a potentially deadly stock of weapons, attacks on Allied troops in the surrounding area ceased at once. It was a turning point at the time, so that soldiers on the ground were able to replace their protective steel helmets with berets. Until then the extremists had exercised a worrying hold over the local community, although it is interesting to note that even as the hard hats were being discarded Buster retained his own protective gear. This included a specially sealed pen designed to protect him from gas or biological agent, into which he would leap immediately on hearing a siren warning of a gas or Scud rocket attack.

Returning from Safwan to Hampshire after the discovery, where for a while he lived as a somewhat out-of-the-ordinary family pet with Morgan, his wife Nicki and five-year-old daughter Emma, Buster was quarantined like any other animal. This in part explains the delay in presenting the medal.

Sadie
Labrador
Royal Army Veterinary Corps arms and explosives search dog
Date of Award: 6 February 2007
For outstanding gallantry and devotion to duty while assigned to the Royal Gloucestershire, Berkshire and Wiltshire Light Infantry during conflict in Afghanistan in 2005.

In a long war against a determined and often invisible enemy, the ongoing struggle in Afghanistan has for many back home been characterised by two enduring images: that of a funeral cortege silently making its way through the streets of what is now the royal town of Wooton Bassett, and combat troops engaged in the painstaking hunt for the improvised explosive devices (IEDs) which have been the cause of so many of those fatalities.

Typically the television pictures beamed back to Britain most commonly show foot patrols sweeping large areas with metal detectors which look not unlike those favoured by amateur treasure hunters. But very often the task falls to expertly trained arms and explosives (AES) dogs, who between them have saved and continue to save literally thousands of soldiers and civilian lives. Such dogs have been an important part of ISAF – the International Security Assistance Force – since the very beginning of the Afghan conflict, and with the Taliban's continued reliance on IEDs their numbers have been allowed to grow even against a background of other service cuts. Many of those recuited to the new 1st Military Working Dog Regiment (formed in 2010) come from dogs' homes and professional breeders, but approximately one third are volunteered for service by their owners much as they were in the 1940s.

Of course not all of those offered are suitable, and while there have been exceptions (including some very successfu mongrels) the best AES dogs tend to come from the traditional gun-dog breeds, such as Labradors and the larger spaniels. Besides an acute sense of smell they also need to be keen on the job, canine workaholics rather than the sort who tire after an hour or two or get bored. For a good one, recruited as a youngster aged between one and three, a typical working life will take them up to eight, at which stage they will be formally assessed for retirement.

Training even the best of them takes time, however, and a process of scent imprinting is achieved over many hours through reward rather than punishment. Typically this will begin with the scent a dog is being conditioned to find – TNT, perhaps, or PE4 'plastic' – being placed in the dog's run close to its toy. Over time the dog associates the smell with the reward – the toy, which might be a ball for it to chase and retrieve – and as these games are made increasingly complex the dog will learn to indicate that he has found something suspicious by sitting obediently.

All the training takes place before the dog is shipped out to the war zone, and to help large-scale exercises are organised in the UK to get the dog used to performing under pressure. Simulating all the noise and confusion of battle, these exercises include real helicopters, radio-control drones, explosions and mortar fire – everything a dog and its handler can expect to encounter in the field. A very few get pensioned off at this point as not 'gun-steady', or find they can't handle the desert heat when they reach the Gulf or Afghanistan and have to be sent home. But in the words of one RAVC officer the majority show themselves to be 'a robust, fast piece of equipment that can work in all areas' and suffer from far fewer technical and operating glitches than many mechanical pieces of military technology.

Once in Afghanistan a dog will typically do two six-month tours of duty, meaning they stay out longer than their human handlers, and while they are assigned to a particular individual it is clear that they also play an important part in raising and maintaining morale among many of the other soldiers they encounter during their stay.

Chiefly they are there to do a dangerous and specific job, however, and it is something at which they excel. For example where time is of the essence and checkpoint security vitally important, a well trained sniffer dog can search eight vehicles in the time it takes a man or woman to do one. But the animals are also highly vulnerable when taking the lead on patrol, and in July 2008 in Helmand's Upper Sangin Valley, with members of the 2nd Battalion, Parachute Regiment, Lance Corporal Ken Rowe (24) and his dog Sasha were killed by automatic gunfire from a Taliban ambush.

The potential for such incidents is always there, but fortunately deaths are extremely rare and most dogs are eventually retired and return home often to live with their handlers. One such is Sadie, a bouncy black Lab who after RAVC training in Leicestershire was deployed in Bosnia, Iraq and Afghanistan. Still working at the age of nine, 14 November 2005 found Sadie and her handler Lance Corporal Karen Yardley at the scene of an explosion outside the UN headquarters in Kabul.

A suicide bomber had killed one ISAF soldier and injured seven others, and when Yardley and Sadie arrived amid the carnage scores of British, American and German troops and medics were tending the wounded and trying to restore order. In such circumstances a well-rehearsed terrorist technique is to plant a second device timed to explode after aid workers and others have rushed to the scene. Sadie's task was to establish whether such a device existed in order that it could be defused.

As 27-year-old Yardley was later to tell the *Daily Mail*, her dog unhesitatingly went to the compound wall on the street. 'She sat down and stared directly into the wall, which meant there was something right on the other side. I immediately shouted for everyone to get out of the area.' The blast wall was concrete and immensely thick, but under the circumstances a handler does well to trust her dog's instincts. Searchers immediately raced to the indicated spot behind the wall, and concealed beneath sandbags found a pressure cooker packed with TNT. As the dog's medal citation was later to note, 'at the site of Sadie's indication, bomb disposal operators later made safe an explosive device. The bomb was designed to inflict maximum injury. Sadie's actions undoubtedly saved the lives of many civilians and soldiers.'

Sadie received her medal from Princess Alexandra on 6 February the following year at a ceremony at London's Imperial War Museum. She has since retired from active service to live with her handler's family in Scotland.

Treo
Labrador
Royal Army Veterinary Corps arms and explosives search dog
Date of Award: 24 February 2010
In March 2008, Treo was deployed to Helmand Province, Afghanistan, to search for weapons and munitions concealed by the Taliban. On 15 August 2008, while acting as forward protection for 8 Platoon, The Royal Irish Regiment, Treo located an improvised explosive device on a roadside where soldiers were about to pass. On 3 and 4 September 2008, Treo's actions detected a further device, saving 7 Platoon from guaranteed casualties. Without doubt, Treo's actions and devotion to his duties, while in the throes of conflict, saved many lives.

In an intriguing development a Belgian non-governmental organisation called APOPO has reported some notable successes using giant African pouched rats for mine clearance instead of dogs. Apparently *Cricetomys gambianus* is easy to train and transport, does not rely on forming a close bond with its handler, and is blessed with an acute sense of smell. These so-called HeroRATS have the added advantage of being too light to accidentally activate a landmine. Since 2003 they have worked to good effect in both Mozambique and Thailand, but so far at least British forces have continued to rely on man's more traditional best friend for this delicate and crucial task. One suspects that if this ever changes Sergeant Dave Heyhoe of 104st Military Working Dogs Support Unit will not be among those servicemen and -women queuing up to swap their dogs for one of these extraordinary rodents.

Then aged 40, the sergeant hit the headlines in early 2010 when it was announced that a second Afghan veteran was to receive the Dickin Medal. The recipient, an AES dog called Treo, had been working with Heyhoe for more than five years after 12 weeks training in Leicestershire and a three-year spell doing counter-insurgency work in Northern Ireland.

Heyhoe described Treo as a four-legged metal detector but was quick to stress the importance of the close relationship between man and dog. 'Basically me and the dog have got to get a rapport,' he told reporters. 'We've got to understand each other and without that we can't be effective on the ground . . . Everyone will say that he is just a military working dog – yes, he is, but he is also a very good friend of mine. We look after each other.'

Apparently as a two-year-old Treo had been a bundle of trouble, which is how he came to be rehomed with the forces in the first place. By the time the pair met up things were very different, however. With Treo fully trained and needing a new handler, Heyhoe admits, 'I looked at him and he looked at me and that was that – I know it sounds daft, but it was love at first sight.' As soon as the two found themselves in front of the cameras at the award ceremony it was obvious what he was getting at, and the closeness between Treo and his handler and pal on the day he collected his medal would have been self-evident to anyone who has ever had a pet of their own.

According to Heyhoe that included many of his comrades, something which serves to underline the secondary but still very important role dogs such as Treo can play – by raising morale within a military unit when they're not actively performing the task they were trained for. 'The majority have pets at home,' he says, 'so Treo being there is an added bonus, although they do know that when he's in harness he is a working dog with a job to do.'

In August 2008 that job involved locating IEDs while the pair were out on foot patrols with the Royal Irish Regiment. In the space of just a few weeks Treo twice alerted his handler to the presence of extreme danger, on both occasions indicating that he had found a 'daisy-chain' by the roadside. A particularly dangerous arrangement of IEDs, this is the name given to a system of linked explosives often strung out across a wide area and designed to explode simultaneously. One senior US general has described how daisy chains are the 'single greatest source of our casualties and remain the enemy's most effective weapon'. For his part Heyhoe is in no doubt that had either of Treo's deadly discoveries detonated the resulting explosions 'would have killed the entire patrol'.

According to Major Chris Ham, at the time of the discovery the officer commanding the Canine Division at the Defence Animal Centre at North Luffenham (where Treo trained), dogs were playing an increasingly important role in Afghanistan precisely because of the enemy's reliance on such devices.

'More and more it is being recognised that the key capability the arms and explosives dog lies particularly in finding IEDs,' he says. With Treo, Sadie and many of their companions providing 'a unique contribution to the troops on the ground searching for these devices on a daily basis' the search for suitable new recruits – particularly springer spaniels, Labradors, golden retrievers, retrievers and retriever-crosses, and larger breeds such as German shepherds – is constant and ongoing. But then it has to be. A decade ago there were barely one hundred dog handlers in the forces, but that figure was well on its way to quadrupling by the time Treo was in Afghanistan, and demand for their skills shows no sign of slowing. As Major Ham puts it, 'if the infantry are out on the ground, then the dogs and handlers are out there in front of them, making sure it's okay to go ahead. They're basically saving lives.'

In asymmetric warfare, he says, 'with the enemy hitting us with improvised explosive devices, there's nothing out there that can find those things as quickly and efficiently as a dog can.' Like Sergeant Heyhoe he knows that in this environment technology often just doesn't cut the mustard, and one suspects – that for a while at least – neither will giant African pouched rats.

As for Treo, by the time he received his medal he was enjoying a well-earned retirement at home with his beloved sergeant (also since retired). There, as he liked to do in Afghanistan, he gets to sleep on his master's bed.

Theo
Spaniel Cross
Royal Army Veterinary Corps arms and explosives search dog
Date of Award: October 2012
For outstanding gallantry and devotion to duty while deployed with 104 Military Working Dog (MWD) Squadron during conflict in Afghanistan in 2010 and 2011.

Theo, a spaniel cross, was teamed with Lance Corporal Liam Richard Tasker of the Royal Army Veterinary Corps and sent to Afghanistan in early September 2010. In his first five months of duty he made fourteen confirmed operational finds, the most an Arms Explosive Search dog in Afghanistan has found to date. During their operations together Theo and Lance Corporal Tasker served in every district of Helmand Province, providing vitally important search support where it was needed most.

The pair's first assignment was working in support of 11 Platoon 1 Royal Irish Regiment, to which end they were airlifted by helicopter into an area in the Nad-e Ali South district where they were to join an operation to search and make safe a strategically important crossroads. Once at the road junction Theo very quickly began to show a high degree of interest in the ground so Lance Corporal Tasker called Theo away to an area of greater safety and briefed the team commander. At that point an armed improvised explosive device (IED) was discovered at the spot indicated by the dog, WO2 Adrian Davies later noting that 'Theo's find undoubtedly saved the patrol from taking casualties or even worse that day.'

On 6 December that same year Theo and Lance Corporal Tasker were again tasked to support the Irish Guards together with some Danish troops forming part of the coalition force. The team were part of an assault group tasked with searching the route leading to a compound building. On entering the compound Theo drew attention to two bags of fertiliser, which could have been used in the manufacture of homemade explosives. Once Theo had found this, Lance Corporal Tasker suggested they make a search the surrounding area and the dog quickly identified a large quantity of components clearly intended to make IEDs. Had it not been for Theo, these devices may not have been found, and it is clear that his actions that day saved the lives of coalition soldiers as well as local civilians from injury or even death.

Theo continue to work alongside the 2nd Battalion The Parachute Regiment in the Nahr-e Saraj district, working diligently to support between two- and three-a-day patrols every day for more than a month. This was in extreme weather conditions and on harsh terrain while he and his handler were frequently coming under constant enemy fire. During this work Theo made several large finds which helped to disrupt insurgent activity as well as locating an underground tunnel and a room in which insurgents were suspected of planning, making and concealing bombs designed to injure or kill coalition forces.

Displaying a natural empathy with dogs and described as a 'rising star' within the Dog Training Group, 26 year-old Lance Corporal Tasker was tragically killed in action on 1 March 2011 after being engaged by small arms fire while on patrol with the Irish Guards in the Nahr-e Saraj district. Theo was naturally with him at the time and on being returned to Camp Bastion that same day he died following an undiagnosed seizure.

Following the tragedy Major Alexander Turner, Officer Commanding No 2 Company, 1st Battalion Irish Guards, confirmed that it had had a devastating impact on the troops. 'Lance Corporal Tasker and his faithful search dog Theo arrived in Number 2 Company to assist us with the hunt for improvised explosive devices - an unseen, arbitrary and lethal threat that kills more farmers than combatants in our area.'

Lance Corporal Tasker, he said, was 'a natural with animals [with] an affection for his dog that truly was a window to his soul. His fortitude and zeal for that perilous task was humbling; it imbued us all with confidence. He used to joke that Theo was impossible to restrain but I would say the same about Lance Corporal Tasker.

'At the most hazardous phase of an advance, he would be at the point of the spear, badgering to get even further forward and work his dog. He met his fate in just such a situation – leading the way that we might be safe. That selfless generosity will resonate among us long after his passing – and must serve as a beacon to all. Greater love hath no man.'

Chapter 5

Fearless on the Front Line

In classical antiquity large and aggressive dogs – most commonly types of mastiffs and Molossers – were trained to attack opposing forces in battle. In the ninth century Irish tribesmen are believed to have set their wolfhounds against Norse invaders. And during World War II specialists in the Third Reich reportedly enjoyed some success in their attempts to train a cadre of 'intelligent' dogs to read, write and communicate in the hope that this would contribute somehow to the Nazis' plans to overrun Europe. The Soviets similarly trained suicide dogs to run under German tanks wearing bombs, but abandoned the scheme after a number of deadly own goals.

More recently the US has also flirted with the idea of using animals as weapons, the Pentagon's more bizarre schemes including pigeon-guided missiles and an elite force of anti-terrorist bottlenose dolphins and Californian sea lions. (Drawn from the US Navy's own Marine Mammal Program, these have been trained to detect and prevent attacks by waterborne terrorists on federal ships and submarines.) As we saw in Chapter 3 Britain briefly considered the possibility of using pigeons to carry small explosive charges or even bacterial weapons in the immediate post-war years, but happily HM Forces have so far resisted the temptation to use animals for weapons delivery or actual combat.

That said, not a few of the dogs employed over the years as regimental or platoon mascots, messengers and mine detectors have stepped up to the challenge nonetheless. Taking it upon themselves to play the fullest possible role in supporting their comrades, some have lost their lives defending the men around them, while others, whether injured in the attempt or emerging unscathed, have earned the undying affection of those they served alongside – and deservedly so.

Bob
Mongrel
6th Royal West Kent Regiment
Date of Award: 24 March 1944
For constant devotion to duty with special mention of patrol work at Green Hill, North Africa, while serving with the 6th Battalion Queens Own Royal West Kent Regt.

Distinguished not least by becoming the first dog ever to be awarded the PDSA Dickin Medal, Bob was a characterful-looking collie–Labrador cross with black ears and a white cap. He saw service in North Africa with a unit which, after a narrow escape from Dunkirk, was reformed to take part in the Tunisia and Italian Campaigns and later the Greek Civil War, which broke out after the German withdrawal in 1944.

Though a mongrel, Bob was an official army dog rather than an adopted stray or informal platoon mascot, and had been sent out as a youngster to North Africa in 1942 after a spell at the War Dogs Training School. Once with his regiment, plucky Bob quickly proved invaluable as both a comrade and companion. Described by an officer in his unit as 'a true and faithful servant', he was soon busy patrolling with the men of A Company and running messages back and forth.

In January 1943 Bob found himself in Tunisia as part of Operation Torch, the Anglo-American invasion of French North Africa. The Allies' advance had been halted at a geographical feature known to the troops as Green Hill, which together with two adjacent areas of high ground – Bald Hill and Sugarloaf Hill – had been successfully occupied by German forces during the first Battle of Sedjenane.

The relatively high German positions meant British troops had to spend the daylight hours on the reverse slopes of their own hills. Any movement during the day on the forward slopes invited shell, mortar and sniper fire, so that it was only after dark that the West Kents could risk moving forward. The result was a stand-off which threatened to drag on for many months, much like the Western Front during the Great War. The much decorated war correspondent and popular historian Alan Moorehead subsequently described the stalemate in his memoir *African Trilogy*, explaining how 'Sedjenane was a wayside railway town in the wet cork forests on the way to Mateur. Whoever held Mateur held [the strategically important port of] Bizerta, and whoever held Green and Bald Hills outside Sedjenane held Mateur.'

While the stand-off continued, Allied troops conducted patrols in attempts to improve their position, harrying the enemy wherever this was possible. According to Bob's handler Company

Quartermaster Sergeant R. Cleggett, it was his exemplary behaviour on one such patrol that led to the award of the gallantry medal to Bob.

A patrol was sent out into enemy lines when we were facing him on that well-known place called Green Hill in North Africa. Bob went with them as a message carrier. It was a very dark and cold night and Bob, who is white, had to be camouflaged.

The patrol had some very hard places to overcome in their job and were soon in the enemy lines. Shortly after Bob stopped and gave the warning of near enemy. The patrol leader waited for a period to try and find out how near he was. As he could not hear anything he decided to go on; but Bob would not move.

A member of the patrol told his leader that perhaps Bob knew that the enemy was nearer than they thought. How true that was became clear very soon after, because a movement was seen only a few yards away. So the patrol left for our lines with some very good information.

In CQMS Cleggett's opinion, 'It was Bob's warning that saved one or two members of the patrol from being taken prisoner and perhaps wounded or indeed from being killed.'

Bob was to remain with Cleggett and A Company 'in every action during our period in North Africa which lasted until July when we moved to Sicily. Bob was there doing his usual job and by this time the weather was very bad indeed, but he carried on [and] you would not think for one minute that he had been under shellfire and bombs.' According to one of a number of letters posted home by Cleggett in 1944 the only thing that got to Bob was the flies, although with the weather worsening as the Allies pushed up through Italy a decision was taken to issue him with a coat cut from an old battledress jacket.

It was in the chill of an Italian winter too that Cleggett and his comrades heard the good news that the PDSA's Allied Forces Mascot Club had decided to award Bob the Dickin Medal after receiving a letter from an NCO recording how he had done 'magnificent work throughout the whole North African campaign; running messages and doing patrol work. Many were saved by his timely warnings.' With his unit still involved in more or less continuous action there was no opportunity for a formal presentation, but a certificate was sent out to the troops in Italy detailing the dog's achievements.

By VE Day CQMS Cleggett was in Austria and, keen to return home, was making plans to bring Bob back with him. Military regulations and a certain amount of red tape looked likely to complicate matters, but after a good deal of correspondence it was agreed that the dog would eventually be able to travel back to England in the care of the Royal Army Veterinary Corps with Cleggett going on ahead.

It sounded a good idea in theory, but Cleggett was clearly concerned, noting in another letter at the time that the pair had not been separated for more than three years. In particular he was worried that the authorities would 'have no idea of Bob and his ways, and that he might get lost'. Sadly that is precisely what happened in February 1946 while Bob was waiting to travel home.

Never taking well to strangers, it seems the brave dog slipped his collar in an Italian railway station at the start of his long-awaited journey and scarpered. Every attempt was made to find him, and his description was circulated around northern Italy via the press and through more official channels. Unfortunately it was to no avail: no trace was ever found of the gallant hound.

Some months later CQMS Cleggett (by now working as a postman in Kent) was presented with his companion's Dickin Medal, but he must have been heartbroken. Today the medal and its ribbon can be seen in the East Wing Extension to Maidstone Museum, together with Cleggett's own decorations (the 1939–45 Star, the Africa Star and the Italy Star) and a life-size replica of Bob DM himself, the West Kents' 'dog of ages'.

F   *a Soldier to recover his .*

Have you seen . . . **BOB**——?——?——?

He is **A LARGE WHITE DOG**
(cross Collie-Labrador weighing about 60 lbs). He has **black ears (white streak on left) and black marking extending over the top of his head.** Black patches show under his coat when it is brushed up the wrong way.

BOB served with the 6th Royal West Kents from North Africa to Austria and was the first dog to win the Dickin Medal for Gallantry.

He disappeared at Milan Station in February, 1946, on his way home to join his master, C.Q.M.S. R. Cleggett, who anxiously awaits his return.

Any information as to his whereabouts will be gratefully received by The Secretary,

P.D.S.A. ALLIED FORCES MASCOT CLUB
14, CLIFFORD ST., LONDON, W.1,
who will see that any information leading to Bob's recovery is suitably acknowledged.

Rifleman Khan
War Dog 147
German shepherd
6th Battalion Cameronians (Scottish Rifles)
Date of Award: 27 March 1945
For rescuing L/Cpl Muldoon from drowning under heavy shell
fire at the assault of Walcheren, November 1944, while serving
with the 6th Cameronians (SR).

Khan, a handsome German shepherd originally owned by a
family from Tolworth in Surrey, was volunteered for the War
Dogs' Training School by Harry Railton after his eight-year-old
son Barrie heard an appeal on the wireless. The call went out
in July 1942 for 'strong and intelligent dogs to be trained for
guard and patrol duty, rescue work, as messengers and mine
detectors', and hearing the broadcast Barrie felt if the country
needed Khan then Khan ought to go.

The six-year-old cream-coloured dog was eagerly accepted by
the school, which from the first identified the dog as being of
considerable intelligence. After training Khan was attached to
the 6th Battalion Cameronians (Scottish Rifles) in Lanarkshire
and shortly afterwards posted overseas with his new handler,
Corporal Jimmy Muldoon.

From the start the pair reportedly established a close bond
and a good working relationship, most of the time being
engaged in routine patrol work while on guard duty. Then, in
1944, man and dog found themselves taking part in the massive
Allied invasion of German-occupied western Europe. The men
of the 6th Battalion formed part of an assault group tasked to
outflank a causeway on what was then the large, heavily
defended Dutch island of Walcheren, before wading ashore
along a mile-long mudbank.

Situated at the mouth of the Scheldt estuary, between the Oosterschelde in the north and the Westerschelde to the south, Walcheren is these days connected to the mainland by reclaimed land and a dam. In the 1940s, however, still surrounded by water, it was a vital stepping-stone to the deep-water port of Antwerp located further upstream, which was to form a vital link in the Allied supply lines. Walcheren's strategic importance – with Antwerp as one of the keys to Europe – meant that it was twice fought over by the opposing sides in the war.

In 1940 the battle was between Dutch and German troops; four years later during the final stages of the Battle of the Scheldt RAF Bomber Command managed to force the German defenders onto higher ground by dropping many hundreds of tons of munitions, destroying a number of dykes and flooding part of the island. Then, at the end of October 1944 in what was code-named Operation Vitality the 2nd Canadian Infantry Division approached the island, planning to cross to it via the Sloe Channel. Unfortunately it quickly became clear that its assault boats would be ineffective in the channel. This meant the only practical approach was along the aforementioned causeway, which was more than 40 yards wide and a mile in length.

The Canadian Black Watch attempted first to send a company across the causeway, but the advance was savagely beaten back. A second attempt, by the Calgary Highlanders, succeeded briefly in opening up a bridgehead, but they too were thrown back, losing 64 killed and wounded in the course of three days before being relieved by another Canadian unit, Le Régiment de Maisonneuve, and the Cameronians. The last named included Lance Corporal Muldoon and Khan, going into action just as Royal Marine commandos landed at the far (western) end of the island in a bid to take out the German coastal batteries.

Code-named Infatuate, this last operation was successful, and within a few days all German resistance on the island had been crushed. But ahead of this Jimmy Muldoon had fared less well. Approaching the still heavily defended island in a small assault craft he and his comrades had come under sustained shellfire from the shore. Eventually a shell found its mark: hitting the boat amidships, it pitched men, equipment and Khan into the thick icy stew of the muddy channel.

As the men struggled to stay afloat and to keep their guns out of the water, Khan fought his way to the bank, where he became stuck in the freezing ooze. Freeing himself he somehow heard Muldoon – no strong swimmer – calling his name over the sound of the gunfire raking the bank and the shells whistling overhead. Some 200 yards offshore his handler was evidently in trouble, pulled down by the weight of his equipment. Khan unhesitatingly ran back into the water, against the tide of soldiers swimming for land, many of them destined not to make it, and grabbing the collar of Muldoon's tunic succeeded in dragging the exhausted and injured man to shore. He then refused to leave his master during a period of recuperation in an army field hospital.

Khan's exploits had been witnessed by a number of men, and when the pair returned to the regiment a recommendation went forward for the dog's selfless behaviour to be recognised officially.

On 27 March 1945, now promoted to Rifleman Khan, Barrie Railton's pet was presented with a Dickin Medal by the battalion commander before a full parade of his comrades. Following his demobilisation Jimmy Muldoon wrote a number of letters to the War Office in the hope that he could keep his hairy pal, but the terms of the deal with the Railton family were clear: Khan was a pet; his war service was to be tempo-rary; and in due course the German shepherd returned to Tolworth and a quieter life.

The two were eventually to be reunited, however, when the civilian Jimmy Muldoon received a letter from young Barrie asking if he would like to lead his erstwhile comrade in a parade taking place on 25th July 1947. As part of the National Dog Tournament, Rifleman Khan and 15 other Dickin Medal recipients had been invited to march before several thousand spectators.

Muldoon leapt at the opportunity, and indeed so did Khan when he entered the tournament arena and saw his old mucker for the first time in nearly two years. To everyone watching and cheering from the stands the bond between the two was impossible to ignore, and after a brief discussion within the Railton family Rifleman Khan was handed over to Jimmy Muldoon and the two friends returned to Scotland together.

Barrie Railton and Rifleman Khan

Brian
German shepherd–collie cross
Date of Award: 26 April 1947

This patrol dog was attached to a Parachute unit forming part of the 13th Battalion, Airborne Division. He landed in Normandy with them and, having done the requisite number of jumps, became a fully qualified Paratrooper.

Number 126 was an unusual lot in the September 2006 auction at Dix Noonan Webb, in central London, of important British and empire medals from the Ron Penhall Collection. A mint-condition Dickin Medal – estimated at £8,000–12,000 – was being sold with its original double-ring collar suspension, correct investiture hook and coloured riband. Inscribed on the reverse was: '"Brian", 13th Btn. Airborne Division, Normandy, June 1944, A.F.M.C. No. 1211, D.M. No. 48'.

Brian, also known as Bing, was a compact cross-bred Alsatian, born in 1942 in Nottingham and noticeably the smallest of a large litter. Acquired by Miss Betty Fetch as a present for her parents, Brian was subsequently sent on loan to the Army War Dog Training School when his appetite threatened to outgrow the family's meat ration. Trained for patrol duties in 1944, as War Dog 2720/6871 he was then posted to the 13th (Lancashire) Parachute Battalion, placed under the command of Sergeant Ken Bailey, late of the Royal Army Veterinary Corps, and selected for parachute training with a scout and sniper unit.

Detailed to take part in the D-Day landings, Brian's two-week training course included ground-based exercises in an American Douglas C-47 Skytrain or Dakota. This involved the troop transport aircraft taxiing at speed and running its engines on full throttle to simulate the noise and movement of an actual drop and the rush of air experienced on jumping from the aircraft. Dogs like

Brian, fitted with special parachute harnesses, learned to recognise that when the engines throttled back a jump was imminent.

During the training course it was established that dogs could not safely exit the plane using the usual side door. Being markedly lighter than a fully equipped paratrooper a dog ran the risk of being hurled back against the fuselage by the slipstream effect. Because of this Brian was retrained in an Armstrong Whitworth Albemarle, a flawed medium bomber which after conversion to paratroop transport took part in many significant airborne assaults including the invasions of Sicily and Normandy and Operation Market Garden.

With a floor exit situated at the rear this required a completely different approach to jumping, but after satisfying the unit's instructors Brian was ready for his first flight – a series of short circuits around RAF Netheravon in Wiltshire – and his first jump, which took place on 3 April 1944. One of only three dogs to complete the course, in all Brian made seven such jumps, each time emerging from under his chute with a cheerful wagging tail.

After a short spell at RAF Brize Norton with the rest of the 13th Battalion, the three dogs then took part in the D-Day landings, being dropped at 00.50 on 7 June over the town of Ranville. Unfortunately one disappeared without trace; the second was badly injured on landing; while Brian himself landed in a tree and came under fire from a German sniper before being cut down by Sergeant Bailey.

With Ranville a strategically important target (for the Germans the crossing on the River Orne provided the only place for a flanking attack on the beaches to the east) the sniper fire was fully expected. Over the coming months the pair experienced further combat, including mortar and shellfire, during which Brian was lightly wounded in the head and eye but continued to support the Allied push by performing a range of sniffer and guard dog duties.

Sent back to England in September for a period of rest (in quarantine), Brian was returned to his unit in March 1945 to take part in Operation Varsity, the crossing of the Rhine by a combined Anglo-American force on 24 March 1945. As well as being the last airborne operation of the war, involving more than 16,000 paratroopers and several thousand aircraft, Varsity was the largest single airborne operation in history to be conducted on a single day and at one location.

After the successful conclusion of the European war Brian remained on active military duty until April 1946, mostly guarding airfields and ammunition dumps in occupied Germany. In the words of an RAVC officer, always an obedient dog who could be relied upon to respond 'to words of command at once', an attempt was made to persuade Miss Fetch to permit Brian to remain in Germany with the army. This she refused to do, and after a period back in quarantine – during which time scarring from several minor wounds was noted – the dog returned to his owner and an altogether quieter life, much of it spent chasing postmen, despite all those years surrounded by men in uniform.

In the spring of 1947 Brian and his owner were invited to PDSA headquarters, then in Cork Street, Mayfair. At a brief ceremony Air Chief Marshal Sir Frederick Bowhill presented Brian with a Dickin Medal. An Allied Forces Mascot Club certificate, dated 26 April 1947, recognised what it termed his 'excellent patrol work and qualifying as a paratrooper, Airborne Division, in Normandy, June 1944'.

In 2006 that same certificate was included in the sale in London, and together with a collection of letters and photographs telling his remarkable story the dog's medal exceeded the estimate by a handsome margin with a hammer price of £13,000. Brian himself, following his death in 1955 at the age of 13, was buried at the Ilford PDSA Animal Cemetery, and is today commemorated in a small display at the Imperial War Museum, Duxford.

Air Chief Marshall Sir Frederick Bowhill presenting the medal to Brian, owned by Miss Betty Fetch

Antis
German Shepherd
Date of Award: 28 January 1949

Owned by a Czech airman, this dog served with him in the French Air Force and Royal Air Force from 1940 to 1945, both in North Africa and England. Returning to Czechoslovakia after the war, he substantially helped his master's escape across the frontier when, after the death of Jan Masaryk, he had to fly from the Communists.

Making the transition from mascot to valued companion to stowaway to symbol of courage for airmen fighting in exile for their defeated homeland, Antis – and the Czech airman Václav Robert Bozděch – would provide the inspiration for a thrilling if at times scarcely believable movie.

Bozděch managed to flee the Nazi invasion and partition of Czechoslovakia in 1939, escaping through Poland to fight alongside the French (initally in the Foreign Legion) before travelling to Britain, where like many of his countrymen the 27-year-old joined the Royal Air Force. Serving as an air gunner, at the war's end he was able to return to his beloved country, only to have to flee again when the communists gained control. This time escaping to Germany (now occupied by the Allied powers), he rejoined the RAF for a second tour of duty.

What makes his exciting story truly unique, however, was his choice of companion throughout all this: a German Shepherd called Antis, said to have been rescued by him as a French puppy after the airman was forced down in no-man's-land during his first spell with the Royal Air Force in March 1940. While the precise details are vague – one 1942 newspaper report says he found the puppy in a derelict farmhouse, another later one that he bought it from a farmer – Bozděch was apparently able to circumvent quarantine regulations, perhaps due to the chaos of wartime, and bring the puppy back to England.

Thereafter the two were inseparable, Antis even joining the airman on his bombing raids across occupied Europe as part of 311 Czechoslovak Squadron. According to Bozděch's biographer, the Scottish author Hamish Ross, he never intended the dog to fly. Instead, as Ross told listeners to Radio Praha in March 2011, it happened initially only because Antis decided to stow aboard Bozděch's Wellington, C for Cecilia when it took off from RAF Honnington in Suffolk.

Before one mission Bozděch was surprised to find that Antis was not waiting to see him off and just assumed the dog was in somebody's hut and wasn't worried. As the plane was crossing the Dutch coast at about 12,000 [feet] he felt this tap at his elbow. He thought it was the navigator asking for a radio fix on their position, but when he looked in his direction, he saw the navigator was busy in his charts. So he stared into the darkness and couldn't believe it, it was the dog, lying on the floor, his sides heaving as he was struggling to breathe.

Sharing the airman's oxygen mask it was a difficult flight in many ways, with heavy flak from the enemy and electric storms that interrupted radio communications. The six-man crew survived, however, and firmly convinced that Antis had brought them luck, decided then and there that the dog should become Crewman No.7.

Taking a dog up in the Wimpy (as the twin-engined bombers were affectionately known) contravened any number of regulations, but the crew were not to be dissuaded and in all Antis joined them for around 30 sorties. On at least three occasions over Kiel and Hanover the dog sustained injuries, but only once seriously. All three times Antis refused to panic, however, his training and natural sense of discipline enabling him to remain calm until the aircraft returned to base.

Eventually the secret leaked out, although members of 311 Squadron refused to confirm the rumours. Fortunately by the time the breach became more widely known Antis was no longer on active duty. Instead the story of the dog who repeatedly chose to share the perils of fighting men served as an inspiring story to anyone with even a passing acquaintance with anti-aircraft fire, enemy interceptors and the noise and chaos of aerial combat.

With the defeat of Hitler, the airman and his compatriots were able to return home, and Antis went with them. Unfortunately their joy was to be short-lived, and by 1948 with the communists in control, Bozděch found himself *persona non grata* and forced to flee once more. For practical reasons he had to leave his wife and baby son Jan, but he took Antis with him, convinced that with the dark days returning the dog would be an useful companion. In this he was soon proved correct, Antis successfully warning Bozděch and two companions of an ambush on the border with West Germany. Several others were killed or wounded on a roundabout but much safer route. Neither saw Czechoslovakia again, Bozděch subsequently remarrying and remaining in England until his death in 1980.

In January 1949 it was announced that the dog's sterling service, inspirational courage and steadfastness were to be recognised, a new Dickin Medal being struck in his name and pinned to his collar by Field Marshal Lord Wavell, who addressed his speech of thanks to the dog personally. Antis soldiered on until 11 August 1953, and following his interment at Ilford with full military honours Bozděch made no attempt to replace this unique animal.

More than 40 years later, in a sale at Sotheby's in London, the romance and sheer drama of their life together was retold once more, resulting in a successful bid of £18,400 for this most unusual Dickin Medal.

Unnamed
Pigeon No. DD 43. Q 879
Australian Army Signal Corps
Date of award: February 1947
During an attack by Japanese on a US Marine patrol on Manus Island, pigeons were released to warn headquarters of an impending enemy counter-attack. Two were shot down but DD 43 despite heavy fire directed at it reached HQ with the result that enemy concentrations were bombed and the patrol extricated.

*

For a Dickin Medal recipient to have no known name is a sad thing, but such was the misfortune for at least two birds in the service of the Australian Army Signal Corps – a blue bar cock known only as DD 43. T 139 (see page 50) and this one, DD 43. Q 879, a blue chequer cock.

At a time when Australia was facing the very real threat of a Japanese invasion, the work of these and other homing pigeons was to prove crucial. In 1942 a review of the existing communications network had revealed a number of potentially disastrous weaknesses in the country's home defences. To compensate for these the authorities were keen to establish a pigeon service of their own, believing it to be a relatively cost-effective solution which would provide quick, reliable and confidential communications while remaining secure from enemy action.

The result was the Australian Corps of Signals Pigeon Service, the nucleus of which comprised wherever possible service personnel who had been pigeon fanciers in peacetime. As in the United Kingdom an appeal went out to other hobbyists in the hope they would volunteer birds, and over the course of 1942 and 1943 more than 13,500 birds were sent in to be housed in lofts in Victoria, New South Wales, Queensland and Western Australia. Their role initially was to provide links between strategically important coastal sites and observation points and the relevant maritime and airborne authorities. Very soon this was extended, however, when it was recognised that the birds could also prove invaluable in the sort of jungle warfare in which Australian troops were then engaged against the Japanese.

To this end Captain Bert Cornish was assigned to expand the service and its overseas field operations, and it is interesting to note that in the post-war years many of his recruits became champion pigeon breeders and racers.

Following their success in pushing back the Japanese along the

Kokoda Trail in what was then the Australian territory of Papua (and in the ongoing struggle in the Coral Sea), the authorities in 1945 recognised that the need for pigeons in this part of the Pacific was stronger than ever. Mobile lofts were rapidly introduced to provide ship-to-shore communication, crucially important to ensure both the maintenance of essential supplies to troops in forward areas and to bring back intelligence from reconnaissance patrols about Japanese positions, potential landing sites and so forth.

The following year, with Americans joining the Australian troops against the enemy in the fierce struggle to take back Manus in the Admiralty Islands, birds from many of these lofts were then hastily reassigned to the American 6th Army.

In April 1943 US Marines on Manus dispatched a reconnaissance patrol to the strategically important settlement of Drabito to assess the enemy's strength and positions. Attempting to return, the patrol came under attack from a handful of well-armed Japanese defenders, and knowing that a counter-attack by as many as 500 enemy troops was imminent, its members needed to get a message back to headquarters. Unfortunately the patrol's radio set had been damaged during the ambush, so a couple of pigeons were released carrying identical messages warning of the attack. Both were immediately shot down by the Japanese and killed but during a brief lull in the fighting a third – DD 43. Q 879 – was sent up. Managing to avoid the fire directed at it from the ground, the bird succeeded in delivering the message to US headquarters more than 30 miles away and within just 47 minutes.

As a result of this timely warning, American planes were sent to bomb Drabito, thereby forcing the enemy to withdraw and allowing the reconnaisance force to return home safely. The bird's contribution to the operation was subsequently acknowledged in a memo from the chief signal officer of the American Forces in the South West Pacific Area to his Australian opposite number.

'The cooperative action taken by your Office in furnishing pigeon communications for the United States troops during recent operations is greatly appreciated,' he wrote. 'Reports from the field indicate that the value of pigeons as an auxiliary means of communication has been established on a firm basis of successful flights performed. The birds, equipment and personnel furnished from Australian sources have proved of the highest value in this respect.'

It took another two years for similar recognition to come from the UK, however, but in July 1947 in Melbourne the bird was one of two presented with the Dickin Medal by the Honourable Cyril Chambers, minister for the army. Among those in the room at the time was Mr A. J. Flavell, a pigeon fancier of Elwood, Victoria, who had donated the bird when the call for volunteers had first gone out.

The medals and accompanying certificates eventually found their way into the official Australian War Memorial in Canberra, where they remain to this day. There it is recorded that 'the pigeons of these lofts were called upon to operate under conditions which probably no other Army pigeons had to endure. At times the birds had to rise 2,000 feet in a distance of three miles, with torrential rain or mist a distinct possibility. Rarely was a message not delivered.'

Sadly, however, none of the Australian birds lived long enough to enjoy the rewards that were their due. Despite their courage and contributions, strict quarantine laws meant that birds flown in New Guinea and the other islands could not be brought back into Australia. Leaving them to fly wild in an alien environment would have been cruel, and so all but six were destroyed at the end of the war. The six reportedly made it back to Australia, but only to meet a similar fate shortly after their arrival.

Sergeant Gander
Newfoundland Mascot of the Royal Rifles of Canada
Date of Award: 27 October 2000

For saving the lives of Canadian infantrymen during the Battle of Lye Mun on Hong Kong Island in December 1941. On three documented occasions Gander, the Newfoundland mascot of the Royal Rifles of Canada, engaged the enemy as his regiment joined the Winnipeg Grenadiers, members of Battalion Headquarters C Force and other Commonwealth troops in their courageous defence of the Island. Twice Gander's attacks halted the enemy's advance and protected groups of wounded soldiers. In a final act of bravery the war dog was killed in action gathering a grenade. Without Gander's intervention many more lives would have been lost in the assault.

Remarkable enough to rekindle interest in the Dickin Medal after a long hiatus (and to become the subject of a moving biogaphy, *Sergeant Gander: A Canadian Hero* by Robyn Walker), this bear-like 60-kilo canine received the award following a long campaign by supporters and many decades after he saw action in the Far East.

Donated to C Company The Royal Rifles in 1940 by the Hayden family, the gigantic black Newfoundland had first attracted the attention of the authorities by his alarming habit of chasing moving aeroplanes down the local airstrip where his owner worked. Very soon afterwards it was decided that he had become too boisterous to remain with a young family, and he was volunteered for military service.

Originally called Pal, he was renamed Gander by his new comrades in arms when they were moved to a new billet at RCAF Station Gander. It was a somewhat dull posting, apparently, at what is now Canada's Gander International Airport;

but the dog settled in immediately and was soon eating, sleeping and even showering with his new platoon.

In October, when C Company was shipped out to Hong Kong, their mascot went with them, having already been promoted to sergeant by the men, presumably more as a sign of affection than of respect. The move to Hong Kong by nearly 2,000 Commonwealth troops was part of a somewhat belated move to reassure the local Chinese that London was actively interested in defending the colony. Barely a year earlier the size of the garrison had been reduced dramatically to the merely symbolic strength, apparently in the belief that Hong Kong itself could not long be defended against a concerted Japanese onslaught.

As part of what was called C Force, the Canadians found themselves under attack almost immediately, what became known as the Battle of Hong Kong commencing less than eight hours after the devastating raid on Pearl Harbor on 7 December 1941. British, Canadian and Indian forces, commanded by Major General Christopher Maltby and supported by the local Volunteer Defence Corps mounted a strong resistance, but against a numerically vastly superior invader – the defenders were outnumbered by nearly four to one – their lack of recent battle experience told.

The men fought bravely, however, but were also hindered by a lack of air support, the colony relying on a five lightly armed biplanes (two of them flying boats) with the nearest RAF fighter squadron 1,400 miles away at Kota Bharu in Malaya. Four of the planes were destroyed in a raid by a dozen Japanese bombers, after which RAF personnel joined the troops on the ground, ignoring leaflets dropped by the Japanese demanding an immediate surrender.

December 13 found Gander, his handler Fred Kelly and C Company at Lye Mun, a defensive position covering an obvious crossing point for Japanese ground troops attacking from the mainland across a narrow strip of water called Lye Mun Passage. A full week of what the official record describes as 'heavy and accurate enemy shelling' was taking its toll, both in terms of casualties and on the men's nerves. Gander too was taking it badly, frequently holing up in a pillbox in a bid to escape the noise, although he was able to overcome his fear to go out on sniper patrols when required.

Following the rejection of a second call to surrender, the Japanese commander General Sakai announced that on the 18th his men would overrun Hong Kong island, and an assault comprising all three Japanese regiments was duly launched across the Lye Mun Passage.

Speaking years later, Canadian Rifleman Sidney Skelton recalled 'swarms of small, shrieking men' pouring off the attacking barges, C Company pouring fire down onto them until their weapons were hot to the touch but the Japanese showing no fear or sign that they might withdraw. Gander suddenly seemed to be in his element, twice rushing the enemy, barking and biting, snarling and rising up on his hind legs like the black bear he so closely resembled. The dog, according to another rifleman, 'seemed to hate the Japanese on sight. He growled and ran at the enemy soldiers, biting at their heels.'

To everyone who witnessed this it seemed incredible that the Japanese did not simply shoot the dog down. Perhaps they were just too surprised to take effective action. In any event, free to harry them in this way, Gander did everything he could to repel the Japanese, chasing many of them into the undergrowth and giving his comrades time to regroup and reload.

By 19 December – exhausted and with many wounded among them – the Canadians found themselves pinned down and under repeated attack from Japanese grenades. The more able-bodied were able to hurl some of these back, but when one landed among a group of seven injured soldiers Gander rushed in. Gathering the live grenade in his mouth, he rushed the enemy in what could only be a fatal exploit, but one which, beyond doubt, saved seven men's lives.

After the battle and the loss of Hong Kong, Sergeant Gander's death was officially recorded alongside the 558 men and officers 'Killed or Missing in Action or Died of Wounds as Occurring on December 19, 1941'.

His story might have ended there, something to be shared by the men he served alongside. In the 1990s, however, a campaign in Canada to have his actions officially recognised began to gather steam, perhaps attracting additional attention as the same action which had seen the death of Gander had resulted in the award of Canada's first Victoria Cross of World War II. Eventually a number of eye-witness accounts and other documents were presented to PDSA in the belief that the striking of a new PDSA Dickin Medal was in order.

Although no such request had been successful for a full half-century, the research into Gander's story made compelling reading and it was clearly well received back in Britain. Most obviously the tale of Lye Mun and the men who died there exemplified what the charity described as 'the heroism displayed by the many animals who served alongside British and Commonwealth forces during the Second World War'. Accordingly, on 27 October 2000, with his old pal Rifleman Fred Kelly in attendance, Gander's actions that day received their long-overdue recognition with the presentation of a posthumous Dickin Medal at the British High Commission in Ottawa. Fred Kelly, who has since died, described the occasion as the happiest day of a long life.

Chapter 6

Counting Them All Out

When Allied aircraft were shot down over enemy territory or forced to ditch in the sea, the lives of crew members – many of them young men barely out of school – more often than not depended on homing pigeons rather than the communications technology carried on board. Birds were routinely taken in pairs on each sortie for just such an eventuality, the RAF eventually training a total of more than 800,000 of them by the war's end. Time and again, when long-distance radio communication was impossible or impractical, or simply too dangerous for a crew stranded behind or close to enemy lines, birds would be used to carry vital SOS messages back to base.

The challenges faced by these birds were often formidable, not merely in terms of the distances they were required to navigate but also because of the additional hazards of flying through a combat zone. At least one bird, Sam from a bomber squadron in Linton-on-Ouse flying Handley Page Halifaxes, is known to have survived after losing his beak to a piece of shrapnel. That said, electrical storms, heavy rain, thick cloud and the like were frequently the biggest problems these birds encountered, and as recently as 2004 a former airman from Bomber Command described his own rescue in a letter to the *Daily Telegraph* where grim weather was definitely a factor.

The writer's Armstrong Whitworth Whitley had crashed on Foula, the most westerly island in Shetland. Two birds were released as per plan, but delivery of the message took slightly longer than expected because, as a meterologist explained once the crew was safely back at RAF Wick on the mainland in Caithness, 'The birds would not negotiate the cold front lying between Foula and Wick, and would have flown round it, via Holland.' With 'no motorways or roads to aid them, just oceans of North Sea', it is hard not to be impressed. Today it is impossible to know just how many Allied airmen's lives were saved in this way, although it is likely to be a very substantial number with one semi-official RAF estimate suggesting that one in every seven of its crew men who were rescued after being forced to ditch owed his life to a message delivered by pigeon.

The first of many hundreds of such incidents in which a crew was forced down over water is known to have occurred as early as February 1942. On that occasion the crew of a badly damaged Bristol Beaufort twin-engined torpedo bomber was picked up some 120 miles out to sea after being forced to ditch en route back from a raid on Norway. By then the birds of the National Pigeon Service had been operational for something over two years, initially as a small Air Ministry section but subsequently as a service department of its own.

For the pigeoneers themselves the fledgling service was very much a learning experience, however, and old Pathé newsreels exist showing personnel at RAF Calshot on the river Solent testing and assessing various different ways to release the birds from planes as new aircraft designs came into service. It was something of a novelty for the pilots too, and indeed the commander of that Beaufort later admitted, 'Things happened so quickly we had almost forgotten about the two pigeons and their container.'

Fortunately the wireless operator remembered, and generally, once crews were trained how best to use the birds, the results were impressive. In Lancasters and other British bombers the pigeons were routinely housed adjacent to the radio operator's position, thereby combining an age-old form of communication with what was then the leading technology. American radio men were also impressed to see that while they had to wear oxygen masks at 20,000 feet the pigeons they carried needed no such equipment, and even at 30,000 feet the birds would sit quietly fluffing their feathers to keep warm.

From 1941 the rate of returns (messages successfully delivered) never fell below 86 per cent. Towards the end of the war a review of more than 3,000 different releases of all kinds – airborne, forced landings, ditchings and diversions – revealed even better results, that 96 per cent of all messages dispatched over a six-month period had been successfully delivered.

Winkie
Pigeon No. NEHU 40. NS 1
Date of Award: 2 December 1943
For delivering a message under exceptionally difficult conditions and so contributing to the rescue of an Air Crew while serving with the RAF in February, 1942.

*

By the end of 1941 it was becoming routine for all bomber, Coastal Command and transport crews to take to the air with a couple of bird boxes. Each was fitted with a drinker and food and contained a homing pigeon to be used in the event of the aircraft ditching or otherwise coming to grief beyond the range of the wireless communication equipment.

Examples can be seen in a number of photographs in the archives at the Imperial War Museum, including one particularly clear image of a Canadian airman based at Waddington in Lincolnshire, Acting Pilot Officer S. Jess, a wireless operator on an Avro Lancaster, seen carrying a bright yellow box under each arm. Designed with a snap-on lid to be watertight in the event of a ditching, at one point macabre stories circulated that at crash sites the Germans would search out these boxes in the belief that if the plane had come down in flames they would find inside a ready cooked meal.

It took until 23 February 1942 for the concept to be tested in action for the first time, when the Beaufort of 42 Squadron mentioned above took off at 14.40 from RAF Sumburgh, located at the southern tip of the Shetland archipelago.

The crews of Sumburgh's torpedo strike aircraft (known as Torbeaus) were usually tasked with coastal raids on Axis shipping off the coast of Norway and elsewhere in a broad stretch of the North Sea. On this occasion the Beaufort suffered an engine failure returning from Norway and after an uncontrollable dive crashed into the sea approximately one hundred miles east of the Firth of Forth. Having previously lost contact with the aircraft, personnel at RAF Leuchars mistakenly believed it to have gone down as much as 150 miles east of Aberdeen. They scrambled a rescue mission but, with no accurate position and only very few daylight hours remaining, the hopes of success would not have been high.

Fortunately the estimate of where the aircraft had ditched

was able to be reassessed the following morning when one of the pigeons – NEHU 40. NS 1, a blue chequer hen hatched in Whitburn – returned to the loft maintained by her owner and trainer George Ross of Broughty Ferry on the other side of the Firth of Tay. Finding his bird at 08.20, Ross immediately contacted the RAF, and although the bird was not carrying the expected message it proved possible to make a better guess at the crew's position based on her estimated time in the air.

Another rescue mission was sent up, and at approximately 11.15 the crew of a Royal Netherlands Naval Air Service Lockheed Hudson spotted a dinghy and dropped a Thornaby Bag close to it. (This was a specialised waterproof container devised by staff at RAF Thornaby in North Yorkshire to deliver emergency rations and first-aid equipment to downed crews.) Having estimated the dinghy's position as equidistant from Aberdeen and Blyth, the Hudson's crew requested an RAF high-speed launch to be sent from each harbour carrying hot drinks and food. A Supermarine Walrus of the Fleet Air Arm also overflew the crew, and within three hours Squadron Leader W. Hedley Cliff and three other survivors had been picked up and were on their way back to dry land.

The fact the bird was dispatched without a message in its capsule is by no means the only fact which makes her story unusual and even more remarkable. It later transpired that while her companion bird had been dispatched with a message attached, the hapless Winkie had been subjected to an unexpected dip in the freezing oily waters around the ditched aircraft when her own box had burst open on impact. Recovering from this she had then set off on her own back to the Scottish mainland, but with no capsule.

In fact a crew member had managed to get off an SOS message before abandoning the Beaufort, but with the radio signal weak it had not been possible to get an accurate fix on its position. Because of this the first rescue mission from RAF Leuchars had been charged with searching more than 70 square miles of water, an impossible task with just 90 minutes of daylight remaining. Instead their rescue depended on a wet, bedraggled bird with oily feathers flying over water in total darkness – something pigeons will avoid whenever possible.

Knowing this about pigeons, and looking at Winkie's condition when she was back in her loft, led Sergeant Davidson of the RAF Pigeon Service to reassess the estimate of where the Beaufort might have gone down. The original search area, he felt, was simply too far from base for an oiled bird to cover in the given time – and indeed so it proved with the dinghy eventually being found drifting 129 miles from base and some 120 miles from land.

Cliff and his crew were quick to acknowledge their debt to the bird and held a celebratory dinner at which she and Ross were guests of honour. The bird was presented with a small wooden commemorative plaque but throughout the evening was observed to be winking one eye. According to pigeon experts this is almost certainly a sign of extreme exhaustion, but since that night NEHU 40. NS 1 has been known as Winkie. After her death she was stuffed and mounted and, together with her PDSA Dickin Medal, presented by George Ross to the Dundee City Council, custodians of the McManus Galleries and Museum.

White Vision
Pigeon No. 3089 SURP 41 L
Date of Award: 2 December 1943
For delivering a message under exceptionally difficult conditions and so contributing to the rescue of an Air Crew while serving with the Royal Air Force in October 1943.

*

Engaging the enemy on something of a forgotten front during World War II, among the important responsibilities of the Royal Air Force Coastal Command was the use of its Consolidated PBY Catalina flying boats to patrol the northern sea lanes looking for U-boats sent out from German ports.

Operating from Shetland, Catalina crews would typically spend up to 22 hours at a stretch on submarine-hunting missions. Their US-built aircraft were well equipped for the task, with long-range fuel tanks, Browning machine guns and up to 2,000 pounds of bombs. They proved devastatingly effective: it was a Catalina that successfully located the *Bismarck* when she went on the run from the Royal Navy in May 1941; and two Catalina pilots were awarded the Victoria Cross for pressing home attacks on other enemy vessels while injured and under exceptionally heavy fire.

In all, these aircraft accounted for 40 U-boats destroyed, but they too suffered their own losses and the second VC was a posthumous award to a pilot of the Royal Canadian Air Force. To limit crew losses as far as possible every aircraft was required to carry a brace of carrier pigeons – not a few of which were bred in Norfolk on the Sandringham estate in the royal lofts – a pair being collected from the base lofts by a crew member each time the aircraft was ordered to scramble. While not wishing to diminish the important role such birds could play by providing companionship, a pleasant distraction or simply by raising morale, their principal task was of course to provide a fail-safe means of alerting search-and-rescue forces should the Catalinas' radios fail following a ditching or other potentially fatal disaster.

In October 1942 a Catalina IV of 190 Squadron set out from Shetland's Sullom Voe base piloted by Flying Officer R. W. G. Vaughan with a crew of ten. After a long but unexceptional mission – and 21 hours aloft in typically appalling North Atlantic conditions – the aircraft was unable to land at its home base because of the weather. Vaughan was directed to Aberdeen and then Oban as conditions worsened. With fuel running out and his options reducing, he took the decision to ditch in the sea and did so at approximately 08.20.

Once down, radio contact proved impossible, so the aircraft's two birds were quickly released with capsules affixed to their legs containing messages giving the crew's approximate position. Meanwhile a search for the missing aircraft had already been launched, but this was severely compromised by the onset of bad weather which prevented any other aircraft taking off.

The Catalinas of 190 Squadron were at this time also equipped with sufficient life rafts for all crew members, but unfortunately on this occasion one had drifted off into the storm with only two men aboard leaving just one inflatable behind for the remaining nine. Given the prevailing conditions, which were so rough that a conventional sea search would almost certainly be ruled out, the nine men decided their best chance lay with the birds. Accordingly they opted to remain with the stricken aircraft in the hope that one of their two SOS messages would get through.

In the event, and in truly terrible conditions, one bird was never seen again. The second – White Vision, a hen bird named because of her colour – battled against gale-force headwinds and rain, low cloud and visibility down to near-zero attempting to reach home across heavy seas. Battered, exhausted and with much of her once-white plumage missing after an estimated nine hours in the air, the bird eventually returned to its loft, from where the capsule was recovered.

The message she carried was necessarily brief: 'Aircraft ditched safely N.W . . . Heavy swell, taxiing S.E. No Casualties.' By making rough calculations based on wind speed, tidal drift and the bird's arrival time, the RAF was able to mount an immediate rescue attempt, and some 40 hours after Vaughan's decision to ditch came news that a fast launch had at last spotted the aircraft off the Hebrides and established contact with its now-desperate crew. It was clear that time was fast running out, and in the event the plane disappeared beneath the surface just moments after the last man managed to leap across to safety.

The two men who had drifted off earlier on the first of the two life rafts were picked up shortly afterwards in the same area, White Vision was therefore credited with saving the lives of no fewer than 11 men. Later and most appropriately renamed White Saviour, the bird lived on until 1953 and enjoyed a long and well-earned retirement north of the border, where she had been bred by the Fleming brothers of Forgewood Road in Motherwell.

Tyke
Pigeon No. 1263 MEPS 43
Middle East Pigeon Service
Date of Award: 2 December 1943
For delivering a message under exceptionally difficult conditions
and so contributing to the rescue of an Air Crew, while serving
with the RAF in the Mediterranean in June 1943.

Together with Winkie and White Vision, Tyke was one of the
earliest recipients of the Dickin Medal. The bird, also known as
George, was reared in Cairo, apparently of Anglo-South African
parentage, specifically for service with the new Middle East Pigeon
Service. This initially tiny local organisation had begun with just
six birds in January 1942 but grew rapidly under Lieutenant Colonel
Hollingworth and soon had its own large breeding lofts. Based on
the edge of the desert at Maadi Digla outside Cairo, the birds served
the Eighth Army in North Africa and later Italy, also the Ninth
Army and the Royal Air Force during the development of the
pioneering Nomad system of mobile lofts.

Nomad was an alternative to parachuting pigeons into isolated
areas. Birds were trained to leave an aircraft at 1,000 feet and
zero in on a basket or similar receptacle at ground level. From
there they could be collected and, once fitted with a message,
released to fly back to their home lofts, thereby providing a
versatile and secure means of obtaining intelligence from agents
or others located behind enemy lines. It worked well too, and
in one test of the idea a six-month-old hen successfully travelled
500 miles back to her loft, 260 of them over open water.

Particularly in the Middle East, where the roads were generally
poor, the Nomad system often proved more efficient than conventional dispatch riders as well as working well when wires and
wireless networks failed. As a result it was not long before an

effective network stretched from Cairo to Cape Town, and from the Turkish frontier to the west coast of Africa, with mobile lofts operated by the Royal Signals accompanying the Eighth Army.

Typically the birds were able to cover 35–40 miles in an hour, although in February 1943 a newspaper back in the UK cited the example of two birds released at 09.05 checking into their loft five minutes later having covered nine miles with the aid of a following wind. The piece, in Buckinghamshire's *Wolverton Express*, was at pains to advise farmers and all holders of gun licences to 'look twice before you shoot a pigeon' – but the weather often posed a greater threat to these feathered messengers than country dwellers looking out for a bit of extra meat off the ration.

Birds from the service also found their way onto aircraft, where again they were employed for carrying emergency messages in the event of a forced landing or when an aircraft seemed unlikely to survive fighter attack. On such occasions the birds would be hurled out of the fuselage wrapped in a loose paper cone which would only unravel once the 'package' was blown free of the aircraft's dangerous slipstream. Birds were sometimes released in this way when an aircraft was not in danger too, the idea being to give the birds an opportunity to hone their homing skills rather than travelling back to base in a box. American crews similarly released their birds in paper grocery bags, a low-tech solution which nevertheless worked at cruising speeds of up to 375 mph. As the war progressed, advances in radio communications should in theory have reduced the reliance placed on pigeons, although it is clear from many personal anecdotes that the practice of carrying birds aloft continued in the Mediterranean until the end of the war.

Tyke was one such, and on 22 June 1943 while seconded to an American squadron flying twin-engined Martin 187 Baltimore light-attack bombers carried an SOS message after the aircraft was forced to ditch in the Mediterranean. Flying from a point approximately 100 miles from his home loft at Berka (Libya), and in conditions of very poor visibility, the bird was twice dropped in the sea by his handlers but carried on. As a result his crew of four was located and rescued, and again lost no time in attributing their rescue to the bird's outstanding performance at a time when visibility was never better than poor.

In July 2000 Tyke's Dickin Medal, together with the original PDSA certificate, went under the hammer at a Spink's sale in London. Realising £4,830, it not only crashed through its estimate by around a thousand pounds but achieved a higher price than another PDSA Dickin Medal offered the same day; that awarded to Peter, a search-and-rescue collie (see page 189).

Dutch Coast
Pigeon No. NURP 41. A.2164
Date of Award: March 1945
For delivering an SOS from a ditched Air Crew close to the enemy coast 288 miles distance in 7½ hours, under unfavourable conditions, while serving with the RAF in April 1942.

Less likely than many four-legged species to form a bond, close or otherwise, with their fighting comrades, the fact that pigeons were assigned to an airfield or service unit rather than to a particular aircraft or crew means that most birds were known only by number. Many remarkable missions were undertaken and completed in the 1940s by birds with no personal identity, flyers presumably simply picking a pair more or less at random before taking off into the blue.

This means that they were much like the mass of human participants in the war, in that they were called upon to do their bit with neither hope nor expectation of any recognition or reward beyond survival. Unsurprisingly the birds that failed to make it home have gone largely unrecorded. If remembered at all they will likely be recalled as failures even though – for all we know – they may have battled bravely and long against the elements only to fall at the very last hurdle. Given the genuine celebrity status achieved by some animals during and immediately following World War II, it is sad to reflect that very little is known about many of those who succeeded too. These were birds whose exploits were sufficiently impressive to earn them a place on the authoritative Meritorious Performance List, published in 1950 by the proprietors of London's *The Racing Pigeon*. For one reason or another, no details of these pigeons were recorded except for the date of the action and the airfield to which they homed.

NURP 42. R. 3287, for example, twice covered more than 350 miles on the day of its release, yet we know no more about him than what is conveyed by the two-word description 'mealy cock', a reference to his colouring. Another mealy, NURP 42. A. 4708, flew 380 miles in six hours and 40 minutes – a phenomenal pace for any bird – while NPS 43. 34548, after a forced landing by the aircraft carrying him, covered 95 miles in just 88 minutes, only to then repeat the feat six weeks later to save a second crew.

At least these birds survived. Many were badly injured: NEHU 39. 3738, known as Bouncer, was scalped by one of several bullets which passed through both the fuselage and her box before the aircraft came down. NUHW 38. CD. 16 had a potentially fatal run-in with an enemy falcon but still completed a 95-mile test flight in good time and survived to complete another 82 sorties. NURP 41. GMN similarly survived an air release over the Bay of Biscay – from a Bristol Beaufighter, a notoriously tricky aircraft for such a manoeuvre – and despite being injured returned home to South Wales.

But many others died after successfully delivering their messages, not infrequently of exhaustion. Very often birds failed to return from subsequent missions when aircraft were destroyed in the air, and at least once (the famously tragic case of Gustav, page 26) a bird died after being mishandled back at home.

Most extraordinarily of all perhaps, several Dickin Medal recipients have also managed to remain anonymous – most notably the two Australian birds described on pages 50 and 88 – although it is hard to imagine how, when each of them was credited with saving multiple lives. Surely even the most hardened soldier or airman would not begrudge naming his saviour, although some of the names which were handed out after the event were at best a little unimaginative.

This one, for example, like Ruhr Pocket on page 30, was simply named after the geographical feature towards which which his fellow crew members were drifting after coming down dangerously close to the enemy. Prior to 13 April 1942 he too would have been a relatively anonymous creature to all but his breeder and trainer (J. Flowers of Radcliffe-on-Trent) and as such listed in relevant RAF documents simply as bird No. NURP 41. A.2164.

Even now the details of his accomplishments are vague, but then with pigeons as with men there is always an element of luck involved in determining the chances of one achieving distinction in wartime. Released from a dinghy by a ditched aircrew drifting off the Netherlands at 06.20, Dutch Coast carried a message back to RAF Syerston. Located near Newark in Nottinghamshire, the base was some 288 miles from the downed crew, a distance Dutch Coast covered in seven and a half hours under conditions which, as the Meritorious Performance List notes, 'were by no means favourable'.

Probably the aircraft was an Avro Lancaster as these commenced operations from Syerston in 1942, when a new concrete runway enabled the heavier machines to replace the Polish-crewed Vickers Wellingtons and Handley Page Hampdens which had hitherto used the base. But sadly even this is not known, histories of the base today making no mention of Dutch Coast or his life-saving flight, preferring reasonably if still regrettably to tell the story of the badly wounded Bill Reid of 61 Squadron who won a Victoria Cross after taking off from Syerston in 1943 and nursing his shattered Lancaster back from Düsseldorf.

Royal Blue
Pigeon No. NURP 40. GVIS. 453
Date of award: March 1945
For being the first pigeon in this war to deliver a message from a forced landed aircraft on the Continent while serving with the RAF in October, 1940.

When Buckingham Palace received a direct hit from the air in 1940 – one of several, although in this case the King and Queen were actually in residence – Her Majesty's response to the shattered windows and the destruction of the chapel was the much-quoted remark that she was glad to have been bombed as it meant that now she could 'look the East End in the face'. Much of her popularity, and that of the King, depended on their decision to share the hardships of war with their fellow Londoners, and the image of the two of them surveying the damage the following morning did much to neutralise and indeed reverse the obvious propaganda value of this particular German success.

Their contribution throughout the war years was in every

sense incalculable, and came in many forms. One of the least-known examples, however, was the King's decision to volunteer birds from the royal lofts at Sandringham for war service – as indeed his father George V had done during the Great War.

The lofts at Sandringham were constructed in 1886 to house a number of racing pigeons given to the royal family by their kinsman Leopold II, a first cousin to Queen Victoria. The gift was well received, and both Edward VII and George V scored some notable victories with their birds. These included first prizes in the prestigious national race from Lerwick in the Shetland Isles, an event which our own Queen has won, having followed her forebears to become an enthusiastic and longstanding patron of the Royal Pigeon Racing Assocation and a number of sister organisations.

Today the lofts provide accommodation for some 160 mature birds, most of which are raced regularly – they have won literally every major competition – while the remainder are stock pigeons used for breeding. George V's decision to contribute his own birds to the war effort was announced immediately following the establishment of the new National Pigeon Service under the direction of the Air Ministry. In what today we would recognise as a photo opportunity, His Majesty was presented with the official badge of the NPS, an attractive (and today highly collectable) button in silver and blue and red enamel, surmounted by a gilt crown and depicting a pigeon at rest.

By 14 December 1939 the journal *Flight* was able to report, 'His Majesty takes a keen interest in the work of the Service and from the Royal Loft at Sandringham the King's birds are daily sent out on war service. Important messages have already been received by their aid.' The same short news item included a typical episode in the life of one of the Sandringham birds, which was air-released by the crew of a British aircraft when the pilot found himself running short of fuel. The bird arrived in good time, and the message was telephoned through to the pilot's base, although happily the aircraft was able to make land and reach the aerodrome.

On that occasion, as the outcome was a happy one, the reporter was simply left to note that 'as had seemed likely, had he come down in the sea, the pigeon might well have saved his life and the aircraft as well'. Shortly afterwards, however, this was indeed to be the case, and one of the Sandringham birds – the aptly named Royal Blue – is popularly held to be the first bird ever to save a crew forced down in enemy territory.

The truth is, it is hard to know. Royal Blue certainly existed, a fine blue cock officially assigned to an RAF service unit in late 1940. In October the same year, according to his Dickin Medal citation, the aircraft in which he was travelling was forced to land on the Continent, probably somewhere in Holland around 07.20 in the morning. Released by the crew straight away, Royal Blue is said by the Royal Pigeon Racing Assocation to have covered the 120 miles back to Sandringham in a respectable four hours and ten minutes. He was carrying details of the crew's position, and once these were received by the RAF's Coastal Command station at Bircham Newton near Fakenham it was possible for all of them to be recovered.

It took until early 1945 for the Allied Forces Mascot Club to consider the proposal of an award on this occasion, which is curious because a number of birds had already been recognised by this time. The decision was quickly reached, however, and a message sent – by pigeon, of course – from Wing Commander Lea Rayner to the King at Sandringham asking whether he would accept on the bird's behalf the award of a

Dickin Medal. On 12 April 1945 the presentation was duly made, with Rear Admiral Roger Bellairs doing the honours, at the same time that a second Dickin Medal was awarded to the equally outstanding Commando – whom we shall meet again on page 129.

Billy
Pigeon No. NU 41. HQ 4373
Date of Award: August 1945

For delivering a message from a force-landed bomber, while in a state of complete collapse and under exceptionally bad weather conditions, while serving with the RAF in 1942.

Bred and trained at Hykeham near Lincoln, Billy's story – or at least the little of it that has been recorded – is similar to that of Royal Blue, albeit without the regal connection.

In 1941 the bird was based at RAF Waddington, now home to the RAF Air Command's deliberately mysterious 'surveillance and reconnaissance assets', but already in 1942 it was one of the older airfields, having been established as a training base in the early days of the Royal Flying Corps. In 1940 Waddington became the first airfield to receive the woeful new Avro Manchester, and two years later the first to fly its spectacular successor, the four-engined Lancaster.

The latter began operational flying at Waddington with 44 Squadron, Bomber Command on 2 March of that year, so Billy's rescue, which took place two weeks earlier, must have involved another aircraft type. This was probably a Handley Page Hampden (of which 43 were lost by the squadron) rather than one of the ill-fated Manchesters, a now largely forgotten design recalled more for its lack of power and poor reliability than for any notable operational successes.

A blue cock like Royal Blue, and just 11 months old at the time of his deployment, Billy was released carrying a message from his crew following a forced landing in the Netherlands. This took place around 10.00 on 21 February. His flight was considerably longer than Royal Blue's, however, at around 250 miles, and the weather conditions far worse with an ongoing 'gale driven' snowstorm. The bird nevertheless covered the distance in 27 hours and 40 minutes, arriving back at his loft at lunchtime the following day in what was described by his owner afterwards as 'a state of complete collapse'.

Sadly nothing more is known, including the exact date and location of the award ceremony, who presented the medal or whether the plucky bird was reunited with his owner. The location of the medal is also unknown, and one can only hope that it came into the possession of someone who knows the story behind it and can appreciate its singular value.

Cologne
Pigeon No. NURP 39. NPS 144
Date of Award: unknown
For homing from a crashed aircraft over Cologne although seriously wounded, while serving with the RAF in 1943.

An unusual award in that it did not result directly in the rescue of either aircraft or crew, the red cock Cologne disappeared with his aircraft reportedly during a raid over the city of that name on the night of 29 June 1943.

Throughout the war Cologne took a considerable pounding from the Allies with a reported 262 raids all told, the first in May 1940. More than 30 involved only Royal Air Force aircraft, but many others were joint endeavours – including the largest, the first ever 'thousand-bomber raid', Operation Millennium, which took place on the night of 30 April/1 May 1942. A year later the city was still coming regularly under attack from British and Allied aircraft, and 28/9 June 1943 saw an immense fleet of more than 600 aircraft setting out to bomb Cologne once again. These included in excess of 260 Lancasters together with 329 other 'heavies' – Halifaxes, Wellingtons and Stirlings – and a dozen Mosquitoes.

While this was a considerable force the auguries were not especially good. With meteorologists warning of bad weather and thick cloud cover over the city, the Mosquitoes were sent ahead as pathfinders although in the event just seven of the 12 reached their objective. In all 25 aircraft were lost – just over four per cent of the total strength – although by the night's end the remaining aircraft were able to deliver a useful blow in what we now know as the Battle of the Ruhr.

Details of which aircraft Cologne accompanied, and indeed its eventual fate, are sketchy, but what little is known about Pigeon No. NURP 39. NPS 144 is certainly impressive. Ahead of this mission, for example, the cock is known already to have flown more than a hundred successful bomber sorties, and had successfully homed from several force-landed or diverted aircraft in many different locations. After his release in the early hours of the 29th, however, there was no news from either crew or bird, and for more than two weeks both were presumed lost until 16 July, when Cologne staggered into his loft at RAF Bottesford on the Leicestershire–Lincolnshire border. Clearly badly wounded, and with several severe injuries including a broken breast bone, an examination of the bird subsequently indicated that these had been sustained at least a fortnight earlier, presumably at or around the time of his release.

Cologne still carried his message, but of course by the time it was received was of little use and the crew were not located by this means. The bird's fortitude and endurance were nevertheless highly impressive and on a subsequent date – again, sadly, the details of this have been lost – a new Dickin Medal was struck and duly awarded to the bird and to his trainer, Mr W. H. Payne of Nottingham.

Chapter 7

One of Our Agents Is Missing

In March 2010, at an event launching the annual London Festival of Stamps, erstwhile Member of Parliament and former postmaster general Tony Benn relayed the story of how his father, a pilot in the Royal Naval Air Service, had become the first to parachute a spy behind enemy lines during the Great War. The drop was easy enough, he said, once they had cut a hole in the floor of the aircraft. At the drop zone the agent was simply bundled through the hole together with several carrier pigeons. These he released over the following days so that the birds could fly home with various confidential messages about enemy movements and other useful intelligence.

William Wedgwood Benn, later Air Commodore the Viscount Stansgate, was to receive both the Distinguished Service Order and the Distinguished Flying Cross for his heroics, the citation for which included mention of 'a special flight by night over the enemy's lines, under most difficult circumstances, with conspicuous success'.

The use of pigeons as agents' couriers was by no means Benn's invention, however, and as long ago as 1870 during the Prussian siege of Paris birds were routinely flown out of the French capital by hot-air balloon. The birds were then able to return to Paris under their own power carrying tiny strips of early microfilm, up to 20 strips at a time, containing important messages for the besieged citizens. (A few years later, and even more elaborately, the Bavarian army fitted some of its birds with primitive miniaturised cameras, hoping to spy on its enemies in a method later copied by the CIA's highly secretive Office of Research and Development during the Cold War.)

By World War II using birds for covert operations of this sort had become more sophisticated. In order to assist Britain's Special Operations Executive (SOE) agents working in German-occupied Europe an impressively precise total of 16,554 volunteer pigeons were trained over a period of three and a half years to be parachuted into enemy-held territory.

Their work, like that of the agents, was of course hazardous in the extreme, and of that total a mere 1,842 are known to have returned home to their lofts carrying the all-important messages. The Germans were known to have marksmen and even falcons on the coast at Calais specifically to bring them down, although occasionally the enemy showed it had a sense of humour, as when an American bird returned somewhat later than expected to its loft outside Cassino in Italy in 1944. Attached to its leg was a message reading, 'To the American Troops: Herewith we return a pigeon to you. We have enough to eat. —The German Troops'.

Such frivolity was unusual, however. Writing a regimental history after the war, Lieutenant Colonel Fritz Ziegalmann of the 352nd Infantry Division described during the run-up to

D-Day 'very lively enemy carrier pigeon traffic in all sectors of the 352 ID. From 20 March to 20 May 1944 27 carrier pigeons were shot!' In early June, just 72 hours before D-Day, another bird was shot down while carrying a message warning the Allies of a German build-up around Omaha Beach. As a result the Americans found themselves facing what one combat veteran later described as 'ten thousand more German troops there than we had anticipated'.

The vast majority of such birds may seem to us more stoical than heroic, the ones which just disappeared, were lost to falcons or so-called friendly fire, as in one air raid where a breeder lost dozens of favourites to anti-aircraft guns. But this is grossly unfair. Desertion is very rare amongst such creatures, and more likely is that many were simply beaten back by the elements or cooked and eaten before they reached the coast. The vast majority of birds which were released only to disappear will still have battled against often hideous odds and as such deserve to share in the modest acclaim accorded to those described in these pages.

The most famous among the returnees today – in many but not all cases the PDSA Dickin Medal recipients described in this chapter – were dropped under cover of darkness into occupied France. It was a country where covert wireless transmissions were both notoriously unreliable and extremely dangerous for any of the military or civilian personnel involved. Other birds found their way back from agents elsewhere in Europe – particularly Holland, Belgium and Denmark – and much further afield the Indian Pigeon Service used the Boomerang System (similar to Nomad), in which pigeons were trained to fly both ways between two mobile lofts, one to feed, the other to nest.

Inexplicably none of the birds which saw service with the IPS was ever recognised by PDSA or recommended for a Dickin Medal, but using this versatile system a great number of birds are known to have performed superbly. Perhaps surprisingly, many were recruited from pigeon fanciers back in Britain and, once transported thousands of miles, proved capable of navigating across unfamiliar territory, including the densest jungle. They would frequently fly 30 miles or more behind enemy lines after being dropped by parachute or with agents in Burma and Malaya. Logbooks in some lofts notched up more than 1,000 successful flights of this sort. After the war the brigadier commanding the IPS wrote personally to thank fanciers in England and to confirm that the success achieved by his service was 'the direct result of the excellent quality of the pigeons donated' – but medals came there none.

From wherever the birds came, however, and regardless of the theatre of war in which they were deployed, it is still humbling to consider the significance of so much of the information, photographs, diagrams and even film carried by the birds from hostile or occupied territory to our own. Often of immense strategic and tactical value, data on enemy positions, likely actions and much information pertaining to specific German installations – including the V-1 and V-2 rocket bases – came to be known through nothing more than the rapid and accurate flight of small birds carrying even smaller capsules containing brief but significant notes of quite immeasurable value.

Kenley Lass
Pigeon No. NURP 36. JH 190
Date of Award: March 1945
For being the first pigeon to be used with success for secret communications from an agent in enemy-occupied France while serving with the NPS in October 1940.

*

Although pigeons were supplied not just to the forces but also to police, war correspondents and photographers and even commercial organisations, the most intriguing are invariably those given to agents and partisans, even though this merely serves to make it doubly disappointing that in many if not most cases very little is known about the operations and the messages carried back in this way.

Of course little or no information was made available to the public during the war, but the silence continued long after the defeat of the Axis powers with those involved often keeping quiet for so long that it was only after their deaths that even the bare outlines of their war service became known. Very little was known for example about the wartime activities of Viscountess Dilhorne before her obituaries were published in 2004, although as Lady Mary Manningham Buller she had spent much of the war raising and training pigeons for the Secret Intelligence Service at her home in Oxfordshire.

As the *Daily Telegraph* revealed after her death, 'her birds were dropped by parachute in individual wicker baskets to agents and resistance members in Germany and occupied Europe, who used them to communicate with London'. The birds would fly back to Oxfordshire with coded messages strapped to one leg, and these would then be removed and handed to dispatch riders sent from Whitehall to collect them. According to the newspaper, 'not until near the end of the war did the Germans understand what was happening and start shooting at carrier pigeons'.

This is not quite true of course, but what is true is that it was only after the war that their owner 'discovered that some of the messages carried [by her birds] had been of critical importance to the military'. Even then it took several decades more for the full picture to emerge, the Viscountess being very much an old lady by the time she learned, as the paper put it, 'that during the war a party of Royal Engineers had been ordered to destroy peregrine nests on the Coast, in order to prevent these birds from intercepting and killing returning pigeons'.

Like others she preferred not to talk publicly about her contribution to the war effort and stayed silent until her death at 93. Such reticence in all likelihood impressed both her daughter and her husband – the one a future head of MI5, the other a lord chancellor who according to their daughter found 'the whole of espionage slightly sordid' – but it is a continuing source of frustration for anyone interested in the details of the birds' wartime role.

Happily a very few of the birds thus employed have enjoyed a slightly higher profile, one such being Kenley Lass, a dark chequer hen bred by a prosperous hat maker from Stockport in Cheshire called Walter Henry Torkington. As it happens she was not trained by Lady Mary in Oxfordshire, but sent to another NPS member, R. W. Beard of Kenley in Surrey, before being dropped by parachute into enemy-occupied France with an agent. Probably working for MI6 and known only as Phillipe his mission was to make contact with the resistance, and to collect and collate as much information as possible before being flown out to safety in a Westland Lysander. This gawky-looking high-wing aircraft is something of a wartime legend, its short-field abilities making it very much the aircraft of choice for clandestine missions to place or recover agents using unprepared grass airstrips located behind enemy lines.

The jump Philippe made into France was no more than ordinarily perilous, although the agent was then required to make a cross-country hike of nine miles, concealing two birds about his person and to keep both hidden for the next eleven days. (The unofficial advice to agents was to cut holes in a pair of old socks, and to put a bird into each one before putting the socks in a rucksack.)

It was a concern that Philippe was not familiar with birds, and that despite some last-minute training he might fail to give Kenley Lass and her companion the care and attention they required. By 20 October he had obtained the necessary information, however, and Kenley Lass – apparently still in sufficiently good shape – was released at 08.20. She carried a note advising the authorities back home that their man behind the lines was ready to be collected. A second bird, a nameless red chequer hen No. NURP 34. SVS. 402, was released at the same time carrying a similar message.

Now part of the London Borough of Croydon, RAF Kenley was a good 300 miles to the north, but Kenley Lass succeeded in reaching the base that same afternoon and was back in her loft by 15.00. Interestingly the second bird returned home within a minute of her checking in. While the precise details of the mission and the messages have not been revealed, the idea of using birds in this way was thus twice proved workable, and according to the Meritorious Performance List Kenley Lass was able to render a second similar service four months later.

Publicly rewarding a bird for such work was clearly not possible at the time, but in March 1945 – with the liberation of Europe proceeding apace – a Dickin Medal was presented to Kenley Lass for her historic flight. NURP 34. SVS. 402 received nothing, however a close second place on this occasion being considered not quite good enough.

All Alone
Pigeon No. NURP 39. SDS. 39
Date of Award: February 1946
For delivering an important message in one day over a distance of 400 miles, while serving with the NPS in August, 1943.

Hatched in Staines, Middlesex, All Alone, an evocatively named blue hen, was volunteered by her owner J. W. Paulger, landlord of the venerable Blue Anchor Inn which still stands in the town's high street. Dropped with an agent over Vienne in the Isère department of France south of Lyon, the bird returned home within 24 hours carrying a vital message concerning the activities of the French resistance.

The details of the operation are not known, but the drop was made within months of the establishment of the Milice, the infamous paramilitary force created in early 1943 by the Vichy authorities. Actively involved in assassinations and summary executions, and in rounding up Jews for deportation to the camps, its creation was also intended to counter the increasingly successful resistance movement in the area controlled by the French puppet state.

Navy Blue
Pigeon No. NPS 41. NS 2862
Date of Award: March 1945
For delivering an important message from a Raiding Party on the West Coast of France, although injured, while serving with the RAF in June, 1944.

Famously instructed by Winston Churchill to 'set Europe ablaze', the Special Operations Executive was established in July 1940 to conduct small-scale guerilla warfare against the enemy and wherever possible to coordinate and assist local resistance efforts in the occupied territories. Often referred to as the Baker Street Irregulars, after the central London street where it was headquartered, its more appropriate nickname was the Ministry for Ungentlemanly Warfare – although more than 3,000 of its 13,000 operatives were female.

Results were often spectacular, and the courage and skills of its operatives were never in doubt, but from the start it was something of an ad hoc organisation. With no established rules or blueprints to follow, both those on the ground and those in authority were left to feel their way as best they could – and then to duplicate any initiative that worked to good effect. For example the Lysander was not designed to drop agents, but by happy accident proved perfect for this task after it became apparent that its original role, in army cooperation and liaison, had become obsolete.

The first agent to be dropped behind enemy lines was Captain Georges Bégué on 5 May 1941, a 29-year-old Frenchman who had studied engineering at the University of Hull before marrying an Englishwoman and joining the Royal Signals. A meeting with the BBC's Paris correspondent, secretly also an operative in SOE's F Section, led him to Baker Street and after a short training course he was parachuted into Valençay near Châteauroux carrying with him a powerful but very heavy transmitter.

He sent his first message back to London on his fourth day in France, enabling Baker Street to send a further three agents to join him, the nucleus of SOE in France. Without doubt Bégué was a first-class wireless operator, but his mission was hazardous enough without the additional risk of being caught using the equipment – as Bégué soon was three times a day. Transmitters were easily located when in use and very difficult to conceal.

One suggestion from Bégué was for the BBC to broadcast prearranged coded signals to agents overseas: for example a line of poetry – 'The violins of autumn wound my heart with a tiresome languor' – was used to warn agents 24 hours ahead of the D-Day landings in June 1944. Another way of collecting intelligence from German-controlled territory was to use pigeons, 17,000 of which were trained by the Special Section of the National Pigeon Service and then individually dropped behind enemy lines by parachute.

Packed in containers with enough food for ten days, a pencil and a piece of rice paper, the birds came complete with instructions to the finders asking them to answer a questionnaire before returning this with the pigeon. Instructions about bird care were also included ('Water but do not feed on the day of release'; 'Release pigeons before sunset unless otherwise instructed'), but the likelihood is that many were found by the enemy or by collaborators, or not found at all until it was too late and the bird had perished.

It is also possible that many birds were found by sympathetic citizens but not returned. Throughout Belgium and France during the Great War posters had appeared warning civilians that 'all persons are forbidden to open baskets or any letters attached to them or to remove them from the place where they were found. Inhabitants disobeying these orders are liable to the severest punishment . . . Any town in which one of these birds is secreted is liable to a fine of 10,000 to 100,000 francs.' Under the Nazis the danger of brutal reprisals was even greater.

Either way it is thought that only a thousand or so birds returned with completed questionnaires, a handful of these even making a second journey, and three managing to complete a total of three missions before being retired. Even so, it was something of a hit-and-miss affair, and very hard on the birds,

1943: The Dickin Medal, much like the Victoria Cross, is deliberately simple and sombre yet instantly recognisable. Created by The People's Dispensary for Sick Animals, explicitly to acknowledge the invaluable contribution that animals have made to the lives of men and women in times of war, it is named after the charity's founder, Mrs Maria Dickin CBE.

(*Above and left*) The PDSA cemetery at Ilford on London's Essex fringe is the final resting place of a dozen Dickin Medal recipients. Established in the 1920s, in recent years the PDSA cemetery has been beautifully restored by supporters and volunteers with the help of funding from the People's Millions and the National Lottery. Designed as a place of quiet contemplation for animal lovers, the garden reflects the colours of the PDSA Dickin Medal ribbon – green, brown and pale blue to symbolise the sea, land and air forces – and is home to a number of moving memorials to these silent heroes. Many of the animals' graves were restored with new headstones where needed, and a special Garden of Remembrance was designed for the site by Bob Flowerdew of BBC Radio 4's *Gardeners' Question Time*.

1945: A popular mascot of one of the wartime PDSA Rescue Squads, Beauty was an early pioneer in the field of urban search and rescue. Unprompted, the wire-haired terrier took it upon herself to provide a vital service seeking out scores of trapped and injured victims of the London Blitz (page 178).

1946: Judy the English pointer, who became the only official canine POW of World War II (page 3). Facing death on numerous occasions, and coming close to starvation, her magnificent courage and endurance in a number of different Japanese prison camps helped to maintain morale among her fellow prisoners. Judy is also credited with saving many lives through her intelligence, watchfulness and determination.

1947: Volunteered for service in 1944, Ricky was engaged in clearing the verges of the canal bank at Nederweert in Holland (page 58). He found all the mines but during the operation one of them exploded, wounding the dog in the head. Ricky nevertheless remained calm and kept working, providing invaluable aid to the rest of his section working nearby.

1947: Honouring the Metropolitan Police Mounted Branch, three horses – from left, Olga, Regal and Upstart – were recognised for their sterling service whilst assisting officers dealing with the death and destruction caused by the London Blitz (from page 214).

1949: 'Able Seaman Simon' (page 11), hero of the post-war Yangtse Incident which saw a Royal Navy warship caught up in the Chinese civil war. Though badly injured by shellfire, the plucky stray kept the food stores free of rats and worked hard to boost morale among the sick and wounded in the ship's company.

1949 (*above and below*): Having made the seemingly effortless but still quite unique transition from unofficial squadron mascot via illegal stowaway to a powerful symbol of courage for Allied airmen fighting far from their defeated homeland, the story of Antis and Czech airman Václav Robert Bozdech would make a thrilling if at times scarcely believable film. It is one of the most enigmatic in Dickin Medal history. Adopted by Bozdech during World War II, Antis flew with him in both RAF and French Air Force machines from North Africa and the United Kingdom. Returning to Czechoslovakia after Germany's defeat, the dog then assisted his master's escape when he had to flee from the Communists (page 88).

ANTIS D.M.
ALSATIAN

DIED 11ᵀᴴ AUGUST 1953,
AGED 14 YEARS.

THERE IS AN OLD BELIEF
THAT ON SOME SOLEMN SHORE,
BEYOND THE SPHERE OF GRIEF,
DEAR FRIENDS SHALL MEET ONCE MORE.

VĚRNÝ AŽ DO SMRTI

1952 (*right*): Lucky saw service with a Royal Air Force Police anti-terrorist tracker dog team during the Malaya Emergency from 1949-52 (page 166). Sadly, three of the dogs lost their lives during the violent jungle campaign leaving Lucky the sole survivor at the end of the conflict. Her award was made posthumously at London's Imperial War Museum in 2007.

"SAM"
RAVC DOG UNIT
FOR GALLANTRY
DRVAR - BOSNIA
18 + 24 APRIL 1998

2003 (*right*): Sam too was honoured posthumously, having died of natural causes at the age of 10 (page 169). Five years previously he had successfully brought down an armed man threatening the lives of civilians and Service personnel in Bosnia-Herzegovina, and a few days later, whilst guarding a compound harbouring Serbian refugees, his determined approach succeeded in holding off rioters until reinforcements arrived. Like the Victoria Cross, the reverse of Sam's Dickin Medal is typically reticent, identifying only the recipient and the time and place of the action being recognised by the award. With only 63 medals awarded in nearly 70 years, the Dickin Medal retains its pre-eminence and prestige.

2003: Buster, seen here after receiving his award from HRH Princess Alexandra, Patron of the PDSA since 1972. The award was made for Buster's oustanding gallantry in March 2003 while he was assigned to the Duke of Wellington's Regiment in Safawan, Southern Iraq. The highly trained arms and explosives search dog located an arsenal of weapons and explosives hidden behind a false wall in a property linked with an extremist group. Following the find, all attacks on British military personnel ceased, enabling peace-keeping troops to replace their steel helmets with berets (page 62).

2004: Unveiled by HRH The Princess Royal, the Animals In War Memorial in Park Lane, Mayfair marked the successful conclusion of a £2 million appeal. Sculptor David Backhouse created four life-size bronze animals located either side of a sweeping 60-foot wall. On one side of this is a carved bas-relief showing images of the many different animals which have served alongside British servicemen and women and their allies; on the reverse, a line of shadowy silhouettes represents the millions that gave their lives.

2007 (*left*): Explosives dog Sadie's award was made for outstanding gallantry and devotion to duty while she and Lance Corporal Karen Yardley were assigned to the Royal Gloucestershire, Berkshire and Wiltshire Light Infantry during the conflict in Afghanistan in 2005 (page 64). Having 'undoubtedly saved the lives of many civilians and soldiers' the dog has since retired from active service to live with her handler's family in Scotland.

2010 (*right*): Treo, one of the hardworking hero dogs of Afghanistan's Helmand Province (page 68). Two years earlier, the dog had been deployed to the front line to search for weapons and munitions concealed by the Taliban. Acting as part of the forward protection for members of the Royal Irish Regiment, Treo on several occasions located improvised explosive devices on a roadside where soldiers were passing. 'Without doubt,' said the official citation accompanying the award, 'Treo's actions and his devotion to his duties, while in the throes of conflict, saved many lives.'

although like many wartime initiatives it was born of the need to do something at a time when more conventional solutions had been tried and found wanting.

Accompanied birds did rather better, and before long such birds were routinely sent with agents going on assignment. By the late spring of 1944 the SOE was operating on a sufficiently large scale to be able to drop groups of agents into France rather than just individuals. It is thought to have had more than 100 operatives on the ground ahead of the D-Day invasion together with an incredible 6,000 tons of military supplies and scores of pigeons for sending messages home.

Once the invasion was under way the numbers of personnel and birds sent to the Continent increased rapidly, as did the area of operations as the Allied push into occupied territory continued. It was on one of these missions, involving a small raiding party on the Atlantic coast in mid-June, that the pigeon Navy Blue saw action having previously demonstrated his outstanding abilities while serving with the RAF on air-sea rescue duties.

Once again details of the raid are regrettably thin on the ground, although it is known to have involved a small seaborne landing at a point approximately 200 miles from Navy Blue's home loft at Plymouth. Issued in his protective container on 15 June, Navy Blue was released at some point overnight two days later carrying a message since described as being 'of immense value to the intelligence branch concerned'.

Exhausted and injured – by what is not known – Navy Blue was back in his loft by 02.45 on 19 June, whereupon the message was immediately relayed to the relevant authorities. As with other birds sent on confidential missions the award of a medal was delayed until the war looked won, and today Navy Blue, stuffed and mounted, is on display at the Royal Signals Museum.

Flying Dutchman
Pigeon No. NPS 42. NS 44802
Date of Award: March 1945
For successfully delivering messages from Agents in Holland on three occasions. Missing on fourth mission, while serving with the RAF in 1944.

Often in researching this book one has encountered surprise when explaining how more than half of all Dickin Medal recipients – if only just – have been birds. It is true that to the layman pigeons look pretty much alike, and one is hard pressed to find examples of bird and handler bonding similar to Simon the cat and his crew or the sniffer dogs which more recently have been deployed to Afghanistan and the Gulf.

But listen to the men who depended on them, and it is not hard to be persuaded. None perhaps has put it better than the late Lieutenant General Sir John Sharman Fowler, commandant chief of the Royal Corps of Signals, who in underscoring what a vitally important role the birds played over many years noted the following:

> It is the pigeon on which we must and do depend when every other method fails. During quiet periods we can rely on the telephone, telegraph, flag signals, our dogs and various other ways in use on the front with the British army, but when the battle rages and everything gives way to barrage and machine-gun fire, to say nothing of gas attacks and bombing, it is to the pigeon that we go for succour. When the troops are lost or surrounded in the mazes on the front, or are advancing and yet beyond the known localities, then we depend absolutely on the pigeon for our communications. Regular methods in such cases are worthless and it is at just such times that

we need most messengers that we can rely on. In pigeons we have them. I am glad to say that they have never failed us.

Strictly speaking it could be argued that the bird known as Flying Dutchman eventually did fail his comrades, but no more than any other combatant listed as missing in action and then only after three successful flights from occupied Holland carrying messages from agents operating at great danger to themselves. His Dickin Medal is therefore one of the rare posthumous awards, made in memory of the dark chequer cock in early 1945, nearly eight months after the bird disappeared somewhere on the way back to RAF Station Felixstowe from a fourth mission in the Netherlands.

Pigeon No. NPS 42. NS 44802 had been bred by a National Pigeon Service member, E. G. Forster of Walthamstow in north-east London, and was trained at Felixstowe before completing what the Meritorious Performance List described as 'a great many fights' from light naval vessels in the North Sea. Thereafter he was dropped by parachute onto the Continent in March, May and June of 1944, on each occasion with an SOE agent whose messsages he successfully carried back to the coast of Suffolk.

Each flight is known to have been somewhere between 150 and 250 miles, but when called on a fourth time, in August of the same year, the bird sadly disappeared without trace. Today little more is known of Flying Dutchman, and nothing at all about the eventual whereabouts of his posthumous Dickin Medal.

Commando
Pigeon No. NURP 38. EGU 242
Date of Award: March 1945
For successfully delivering messages from agents in occupied France on three occasions: twice under exceptionally adverse conditions, while serving with the NPS in 1942.

*

Said to have completed an astonishing 90 or more missions requiring him to carry messages back from agents in the field, the red chequer cock known as Commando was bred by the well-known Sussex fancier and gentleman's outfitter Mr S. A. 'Sid' Moon at his Mount Loft on the Broadway in Haywards Heath.

Moon had been an Army Pigeon Service volunteer during the Great War, a staff sergeant training pigeons in Ireland for use on the Western Front. Like others of his vintage he was quick to offer his own birds for military duties when news began circulating in racing circles that a National Pigeon Service was to be established. A number of them, chiefly red chequer cocks like Commando, subsequently made it onto the Meritorious Performance List after being dropped at night into enemy-occupied France.

As a successful racing man with more than 30 years breeding and training under his belt, Moon already had a good deal of experience of flying birds over long distances in club events, and possibly even from the Continent. Before long he had scores of birds performing official duties, those who made it back being trained to home to his own loft rather than a nearby military one. The messages they carried were then extracted from their tiny canisters before being rushed to London to be decoded.

On three occasions the four-year-old Commando attracted the particular attention of the authorities, in June, August and September 1942. Each time he was dropped with an agent into France, and each time he returned on the same day as his release carrying valuable information revealing the location of German troops, industrial sites and possibly injured British soldiers. On two of these occasions he did so despite being forced to fly in conditions afterwards described as 'exceptionally adverse'.

To put those performances into some kind of perspective it is worth noting that only around one in eight of the birds so deployed ever returned home, so to achieve it three times is a very singular distinction, particularly when the flights were so long. Clearly an individual bird's ability, stamina and determination had a role to play, so too the skill of their owners and/or trainers. Even then fate could play its hand. Many very good birds died as a result of bad weather, or because in order to avoid it they were forced to fly unfeasible distances and eventually succumbed to exhaustion.

Some may have gone astray after losing their way; others were doubtless brought down by the enemy or indeed killed by natural enemies such as birds of prey or domestic cats. And of those who did return many could not be sent out again, having either sustained injuries along the way or been covered in oil or simply exerted themselves to such a degree that a full recovery was unlikely. It also has to be said that 1942 was a particularly bleak year for the war in France, with communications especially difficult due to unreliable equipment and the Germans ruthlessly engaged in hunting for wireless operators.

Perhaps in the final analysis it is the quite literally overwhelming odds the birds faced that endear us to the pigeons' tales, and which – on the rare occasions that Dickin Medals come up for sale – ensure that those awarded to birds are typically valued every bit as highly as those given to other species.

Certainly Commando's was, when together with a couple of message canisters it was sent to auction by Sid Moon's granddaughter Valerie Theobold in the autumn of 2004. For those who follow such things and enjoy these little footnotes of war it must have been gratifying to see how much coverage the sale got in the press, with the BBC being among the first to offer a rerun of what it called the 'spy pigeon' and its personal war against the Nazis.

For the benefit of viewers and listeners Ms Theobold recalled 'the noise of the pigeons and probably also the smell of the pigeons', while another family member explained how 'it was terribly hard for the agents or for the people who were occupied trying to get messages out by radio because if they were caught they were shot'. Pigeons, he said, 'were one way of getting information back that was crucial'.

Presented to Commando and Sid Moon on the same day that Royal Blue (see page 110) received his, the medal was expected to fetch between £5,000 and £7,000 when offered at auction by Spink in London. In the event it went to an unnamed buyer for considerably more, the hammer eventually coming down at £9,200. Today the buyer is still unknown, but Commando's award is thought to have joined a collection of three other Dickin Medals which its new owner had previously acquired.

Commando happily survived the war and afterwards cemented his celebrity status by taking part in an exhibition of wartime homing pigeons. After that he was put out to stud so that future generations could share in his stamina and tenacity.

Scotch Lass
Pigeon No. NPS 42. 21610
Date of Award: June 1945

For bringing 38 microphotographs across the North Sea in good time although injured, while serving with the RAF in Holland in September 1944.

An unusually well-travelled bird even by National Pigeon Service standards, Scotch Lass was hatched by breeder Collin & Son in Whitecraig near Musselburgh, where the East Lothian Pigeon

Racing Club still hosts the Edinburgh International Pigeon Show. Her training took place at the RAF station in Felixstowe before a spell back even further north – at RAF Wick in Caithness – only for her to be redeployed to Suffolk at her training base.

In the course of her service the hen made a total of 43 flights home from small naval craft operating in the North Sea before being selected for special duties in 1944. In September of that year she was dropped with an agent into Holland, the mission requiring the bird to fly to England with intelligence rather than the details and coordinates of a undercover operative in need of recovering home. Scotch Lass was accordingly released at dawn carrying the material in question, but unfortunately in the half-light she sustained a number of injuries almost immediately after flying into telegraph wires. Seemingly undeterred she got airborne again and despite her wounds flew approximately 260 miles back to her home loft.

Her flight in this condition makes her story unusual, but so does her cargo, which – almost certainly uniquely for a Dickin Medal recipient – comprised a quantity of microphotographs. Taken by resistance workers in Holland, these pictures are thought to have contained intelligence relevant to the progress of the Allies' reconquest of continental Europe. As micro-photographs they would also have contained a great deal of information, far more than would ordinarily have been carried by a single pigeon.

That said, this sort of technology was far from new and bore a remarkable similarity to the aforementioned balloon flights from Paris during the Franco-Prussian War in the 1870s. On that occasion the pioneering French inventor and photographer René Prudent Patrice Dagron, the city's new *chef de service des correspondences postales photomicroscopiques*, had come to the aid of France. By photographically reducing documents by a factor of 40 he made it possible for a single pigeon to carry up to 20 messages at a time. French records show that more than 115,000 messages were carried in this way, each one rolled into goose quills attached to the birds' wings, with Dagron reportedly receiving 15 francs per thousand characters carried.

By 1926 technological advances had made it possible to reproduce the entire Bible 50 times on a piece of film no more than one inch square, and indeed in 1971 *Apollo 14* carried a number of such Bibles to the moon and back. During World War II things had continued to progress, and in the December 1942 editon of *Popular Mechanics* it was even suggested that in their war against the Japanese the Chinese ('always an ingenious people') were sending microphotographic messages using bees.

True or not, by this time it was certainly possible in theory. Using better lenses than the Frenchman had, and improved film, it was already feasible to reduce material to the point where as much as 15 lines of text could be could be contained within a single full stop. Concealed in a conventional letter posted by an agent, one of these would have looked completely innocuous, yet when blown up 200 times provided text that was entirely readable. The potential to work at a similar level of photographic reduction meant that a single bird could transport an immense amount of material from agent to headquarters, either in a conventional leg capsule or a slightly larger one attached to the bird using a lightweight harness.

Unfortunately however no more is known of the contents of the message than of the eventual fate of Scotch Lass herself.

Mary of Exeter
Pigeon No. NURP 40. WCE 249
Date of Award: November 1945
For outstanding endurance on War Service in spite of wounds.

*

Remembered as the 'bird who would not give up', Mary of Exeter was one of the last birds to receive the Dickin Medal. After a long period of service which saw her severely injured on several occasions, she was happily to survive the war. Signed up for the National Pigeon Service in 1940 and on duty until the end of the European war five years later, she made a total of four flights back from occupied France, sustaining injuries on no fewer than three of them and at one point losing part of one wing to enemy gunfire.

Bred and owned by Charlie Brewer, a West Country shoe-maker, Mary of Exeter was one among many birds which he volunteered for war work. Several are thought to have helped maintain a line of communication between London and Plymouth, although like all pigeon fanciers who volunteered their birds Brewer was required to refrain from giving too much away about operations and cheerfully did so.

Mary was housed at Brewer's home loft in Exeter's historic West Quarter, an attractive part of the city located just inside the old walls. Unfortunately what German radio described as 'the Jewel of the West' was to come under attack as part of the so-called Baedecker raids on some of England's more attractive but strategically unimportant towns and cathedral cities. These included Exeter, Bath, Norwich, Canterbury and York, the scale of the destruction relative to their modest size leading some to liken the results to the Blitz.

Said to have been a response to RAF area bombing, in particular the destruction of historic Lubeck, these retaliatory raids started with an airborne assault on Exeter on 23 April 1942. During the attack a massive bomb fell close to Charlie Brewer's loft, killing a number of his birds. Two nights later another attack brought more carnage to the city, a second bomb falling close to the garage or stable to which the birds had been temporarily removed. Mary was fortunately unharmed but escaped from her damaged basket and was clearly badly rattled.

By 4 May German radio was crowing, 'We have destroyed that jewel, and the Luftwaffe will return to finish the job.' One bomber pilot described in detail 'the fantastic sight' of a 'night of terror for the Exeter people', 265 of whom died as a result of German bombing. But through it all the magnificent Decorated Gothic cathedral remained standing, and life for the city and the survivors went on.

For Mary of Exeter the second raid was another narrow escape, but on operations she was to be somewhat less fortunate and in total received some 22 stitches before the war's end. On one occasion she disappeared for four days after being dropped behind enemy lines, eventually returning home with the vital message attached but her neck and right breast badly torn. A matter of weeks later she was back on duty, this time reaching her loft with a section of wing missing and three shotgun pellets still embedded.

Patched up again and allowed a few days to recover, she was sent out once more but failed to return to her loft. She was discovered days later in a field outside Exeter, reportedly more dead than alive and patently exhausted. Yet again she bore signs of having been attacked, this time by a hawk or falcon which had left Mary with a long deep wound from the top of her head down her neck with a number of smaller punctures to her body. As this left her unable to hold her head properly, Charlie Brewer fitted her with a small leather collar and for several weeks fed and watered his precious bird by hand until eventually she recovered.

More than once it has been said that 22 stitches for a small bird is equivalent to more than 4,000 on an average man.

Probably it is no easier to prove than to disprove the mathematics involved in such an equation, but it is surely hard not to admire the strength and tenacity of something weighing just a few hundred grams – and to marvel at such astonishing courage under fire.

Chapter 8

SAS: Special Animal Service

For a nation so famously fond of its pets and animals generally, it took until 2004 for the British formally to acknowledge the immense contribution to the war effort of literally millions of feathered and four-legged creatures. Various private and family memorials had been erected to individual animals who served, suffered and sometimes died alongside home, Commonwealth and Allied forces in the last hundred years and more, but nothing official existed until November of that year.

Unveiled by HRH the Princess Royal on a prominent site towards the top of Park Lane in London, the large Portland stone and bronze Animals In War Memorial marked the successful conclusion of a £2 million appeal. The work of sculptor David Backhouse, the striking monument depicts two heavily laden pack mules approaching a narrow gap in an otherwise inpenetrable 60-foot-long wall. On one side of this a bas-relief features images of the many different animals that served alongside British servicemen and -women and their allies; on the reverse a line of shadowy silhouettes represents the millions of them who gave their lives, while cast in bronze a heavy horse and dog walk on. The dog is glancing back towards his dead comrades, but the pair, it is to be hoped, are seen walking into a brighter future.

The inscriptions on the wall identify the theatres of war, giving an estimate of the numbers of animals lost and observing that 'They had no choice.' Deliberately no attempt has been made to identify individual animals or particular actions, however, as the appeal was expressly conceived to provide a memorial to all rather than to the relatively tiny proportion of heroes whose stories have become more widely known. In particular, it might be said to provide a memorial for the vast majority of animals whose service was anonymous and whose actions remain largely unknown.

Of course the reality is that during any conflict this includes most service animals, the majority of them almost anonymous participants and now even more so as the passing of each generation of service veterans robs us of another tranche of personal recollections.

Inevitably the lack of recognition was more pronounced for some than for others, especially when the animals in question were engaged in covert activities or posted far from home. Then as now a good story needed to be accompanied by an engaging image – and very often it really is that simple – so that the lack of an opportunity or a camera to take a photograph was often enough to prevent the public even hearing of a particular animal's courage, its intelligence or quite extraordinary fortitude.

The irony of this is that today we hear fewer real stories about real animals than we do the details of one or other of sometimes bizarre schemes which emerged periodically from the Special Operations Executive HQ at 64 Baker Street in London or its top-secret laboratory at 35 Portland Place. Many of these failed from the outset, but the fact that they were often a bit bonkers – with a touch of James Bond or Desmond Llewelyn's character 'Q' – means they can always be relied upon to provide good copy when the press dig around looking for good wartime spy stories. Possibly Britain's enduring love of hopeless causes has a role to play here too.

An example of this would be the top-secret 1941 initiative to sneak dead rats filled with high explosive into coal stores on the Continent, a genuine scheme which was the subject of numerous news stories when the story leaked out a few years ago. The idea was that the rats would interrupt Germany's munitions production by blowing up boilers in scores of factories and workshops. However, such elaborate plans succeed only very rarely, and in this case the secret was blown almost immediately when the first consignment of rats sent across the Channel was discovered by the Gestapo.

In truth, successful espionage and resistance work tends to be harder than this sort of thing sounds, and much harder to glamorise. Organisations such as the SOE, the Secret Intelligence Service MI6, MI9 – charged with helping Allied personnel evade capture – and the government's propaganda wing, the Political Warfare Executive, depended more on brave men and women doing dangerous and dogged work than on elaborate schemes; resourceful individuals relying on their wits and common sense, and with little or nothing in the way of clever gadgets.

As we have already seen, pigeons proved vital to such efforts, being plentiful, reliable and relatively easy to train, transport and conceal. They were also fast and generally harder for the enemy to detect compared to the bulky and often unreliable transmitting equipment available in the 1940s. The Special Forces certainly appreciated their value, and as recently as September 2011 the SAS published a hitherto secret diary giving a fascinating insight into why this would have been.

The diary revealed, among many other schemes, a July 1944 plan for the SAS to sneak into France and kidnap Field Marshal Erwin Rommel. Noting the enormous propaganda value of the capture of such a senior German commander, and his transport in chains back to Britain, the single-page report eventually concluded that actually it might be easier just to kill him in France. A successful kidnap, it noted, 'would require successful two-way W/T [walkie-talkie] communication and therefore a larger party, while killing could be reported by pigeon'. As it happens Rommel of course killed himself shortly afterwards, and it is still not known what steps – if any – the SAS took towards carrying out such a mission.

Plenty of other secret operations were successfully executed, however, and in these many hundreds of pigeons played an important role. Today very little is known about some of these birds. Many, including a few PDSA Dickin Medal winners, are not even known by name; in other cases the details of their achievements are so sketchy that one can do little more than describe them in just a line or two while setting them in the context of what was going on in the war at that time.

Operation Gibbon in 1942 is typical of the kind of work many pigeons undertook, a flight over Belgium on behalf of the Political War Executive to establish and organise a secret new carrier-pigeon communications network in that country. The birds needed for this were typically flown across the channel in what became known as Tempsford Taxis after the RAF station of that name in Bedfordshire. This was home to the special duties or Moonlight squadrons – Nos 138 and 161 – which flew SOE personnel and supplies into enemy-occupied Europe.

Some were flown in by skilled Westland Lysander pilots using field landing strips under cover of darkness, while others were dropped by parachute with SOE or SAS units. In 1940 the Special Parachute Equipment Section had been formed to handle the dropping of supplies and men into Europe in this way.

Agents – known as Joes, although a good many were women – were taught special techniques at a number of secret training establishments. Skills included picking locks, undoing handcuffs with a paper clip and learning how to follow suspects without being noticed. One operative clearly had no difficulty picking up these essential skills, although as a trainee with SOE's French Section in London Odette Brown admitted she 'couldn't bear the thought of handling a bird with feathers'.

Everything the agents and their resistance contacts required, from guns and ammunition to miniature radios, printing machinery and of course the birds, were packed into special containers to be dropped at night to waiting partisans. The process was described by one Halifax bomber crew member, Warrant Officer John Charrot DFC of 138 Squadron, speaking many years after his retirement from duty.

In *Forgotten Voices of the Secret War: An Inside History of Special Operations in the Second World War* by Roderick Bailey Charrot describes how 'the pigeons . . . had their own little parachute, they were in a little cage made of cardboard and they had food and some water in there, and we used to try and find a nice quiet spot for these so that they would be all right. We would drop them and watch them go down.' His squadron alone is known to have dropped 39,000 containers and nearly

THE ANIMALS' VC: FOR GALLANTRY AND DEVOTION

1,000 agents – and collected many more – at a loss of some 70 aircraft. However, as many secret papers relating to the special duties squadrons are probably still to be released, the full extent of the crews' bravery and that of the agents is not fully known.

Occasionally even now details leak out. Aged 92 in 2008, champion pigeon breeder Jack Lovell confirmed in a number of newspaper interviews that he had bred birds during the war after being approached by MI5. The birds, he said, were trained at a secret location near Dover, the XX Lofts, but because of the Official Secrets Act 'I couldn't talk about what my pigeons were doing until a couple of years ago.'

Told his birds were being assigned to the House of Commons Pigeon Service – a fictional entity – Lovell was instructed to transport them to London in cardboard boxes rather than baskets. He was also told to use only St James's Park Tube station – conveniently located for 54 Broadway and 21 Queen Anne's Gate, both of them MI6 premises with a secret tunnel connecting the two – but thereafter could only guess at the uses to which the birds were put.

Some almost certainly were used by the French resistance, their messages being passed to Bletchley Park in Buckinghamshire for decoding and analysis. (Now a museum, Hut 8 includes an exhibition of material relating to this.) Others were reportedly fitted with leg tags copied from a couple of Nazi birds which had been captured in the hope that they could infiltrate German lofts and collect enemy intelligence that way. Papers released in 2008 show that consideration was also given to a 1943 plan to drop pigeons into France. These were to carry misleading information suggesting an Allied invasion was due to take place on the west coast. It is unclear whether this plan, part of Operation Fortitude, was ever carried out. Instead, as with the final few remaining Dickin Medal pigeons listed here, one is left with just dates, occasionally a name, and precious little else.

Too often all we know is that in advanced observation posts, where terrain or proximity to enemy lines made it impossible to string an aerial or use a radio, towards the end of the war there was still nothing to beat a well-trained pigeon. Even where equipment could be used, secret radio operators took time to train and were too often captured and killed if they stayed in one place or transmitted for too long. But carried in a basket, in a sling under the arm, or even in a patrol member's shirt or sock, a bird would often get through when nothing else stood a chance.

Broad Arrow
Pigeon No. 41 BA 2793
Date of Award: October 1945
For bringing important messages three times from enemy-occupied country, viz: May 1943, June 1943 and August 1943, while serving with the Special Service from the Continent.

Trained on the estate of London store magnate Sir Ernest Debenham in Dorchester, Broad Arrow returned from Vire and Saint-Sever in 1943. Both areas in the Basse-Normandie region of northern France which were to see fierce fighting the following year with many hundreds of Allied and civilian casualties. A third flight was from another unidentified location known only to have been in France.

Unnamed
Pigeon No. NPS 42. NS 2780
Date of Award: October 1945
For bringing important messages three times from enemy-occupied country, viz: July 1942, August 1942 and April 1943, while serving with the Special Service from the Continent.

*

Another of Sir Ernest's birds, bred by B. Powell of Hereford, NPS 42. NS 2780 returned from the university town of Konstanz in south-west Germany and from two unidentified locations in Belgium and France.

Unnamed
Pigeon No. NPS 42. NS 7524
Date of Award: October 1945

For bringing important messages three times from enemy-occupied country, viz: July 1942, May 1943 and July 1943, while serving with the Special Service from the Continent.

Bred in Barnsley, Yorkshire by C. Dyson, NPS 42. NS 7524 was trained by Lady Mary Manningham Buller (see page 121). It returned to her Oxfordshire loft from three different locations, one in Brittany and two others elsewhere in occupied France.

Maquis
Pigeon No. NPS NS 36392
Date of Award: October 1945

For bringing important messages three times from enemy-occupied country, viz: May 1943 (Amiens), February 1944 (Combined Operations), and June 1944 (French Maquis) while serving with the Special Service from the Continent.

A blue chequer cock bred by the Brown Brothers in Bedford and owned by P. Cope of Duxford in Cambridgeshire. After training by the Army Pigeon Service, Maquis completed a total of four documented flights home carrying important operational messages.

His name derives from the largely rural bands of insurgents who, escaping to the hills to avoid being made to join forced-labour gangs working for the German occupiers, joined forces with the resistance. Initially the *maquisards* were only loosely organised, and operated on a small-scale local level, harrying the Germans as well as members of the Milice and other collaborators while armed with little more than hunting rifles and knives. As the fighting wore on, however, their operations became more sophisticated, and weapons captured from the Germans were supplemented by air drops of guns and explosives supplied through SOE.

By June 1944, and the date of the bird's final flight, communications between French resistance forces and the British secret services were very good, and both before and during the D-Day landings the Maquis was sufficiently well organised and armed to make a major contribution. Destroying railways and attacking German columns as reinforcements moved towards the coast, some were also involved in the heaviest fighting. One group of 7,000 (including SOE agent Nancy Wake, who had been parachuted into the Auvergne) successfully engaged a German force more than three times its size.

Where our bird was dropped (and when) is not known, and like much about the Maquis themselves the mystery of the message he carried on that last flight is now unlikely to be solved. The award of a Dickin Medal suggests it was something out of the ordinary – so many birds flew back from Normandy but received no more than a welcome feed – but one can say no more than that.

Mercury
Pigeon No. NURP 37 CEN 335
Date of Award: August 1946
For carrying out a special task involving a flight of 480 miles from Northern Denmark while serving with the Special Section Army Pigeon Service in July 1942.

*

Bred and trained by J. Catchpole in Ipswich, Suffolk, Mercury was dropped in Denmark on 26 June 1942, returning home with a message just four days later.

The nature of the message is not known, although by this time the country had been in German hands for more than two years. As early as 7 April 1940 the British Admiralty had received a warning that an invasion fleet was steaming towards Denmark from Germany, but dismissed the report as being 'of doutbful value'. By 9 April the Germans had successfully occupied Copenhagen, however, and taken by surprise (and knowing his small country could not resist) King Christian X ordered an immediate ceasefire.

For a while the two countries cooperated economically, and indeed the Danish population of less than four million effectively fed eight million Germans for most of the war with pork and milk from their famously efficient farms. But there was some armed resistance too, from a movement known as the *Modstandsbevægelsen*. Compared to its equivalents in other occupied countries this was slow to develop, but perhaps only because of Germany's decision initially to allow the Danes a relatively high degree of self-government.

The Danes were largely successful in their efforts to get Jews out of the country and into neutral Sweden, thereby preventing the vast majority of the more than 8,000 of them being deported to Nazi concentration camps. Small cells – including one group of eight schoolboys in Aalborg – were also soon busy carrying out acts of sabotage against the Germans and German installations, and although Scandinavians are famously independent it is known that the British supplied them with weapons and explosives for this purpose.

In June 1940 Winston Churchill had asked the secretary of the Committee of Imperial Defence, General Ismay, 'What arrangements are being made for good agents in Denmark?' but it was 1942 before contact was first made with the SOE. Until then operations had generally been on a small scale, and they remained so until 1944. It is possible however that Mercury was parachuted into the country in order to assist with one of the small early groups' intelligence-gathering missions.

As the war continued, German setbacks alerted more Danes to the realisation that the occupation need not be permanent. Growing in strength, size and confidence – the brilliant Jewish evacuation involved many hundreds of Danes from all walks of life – the resistance was able to claim many successes, although ferocious reprisals meant as many as 850 of their number lost their lives in action, in prison or by execution.

Mercury

Unnamed
Pigeon No. NURP 38 BPC 6
Date of Award: August 1946
For three outstanding flights from France while serving with the Special Section, Army Pigeon Service, 11 July 1941, 9 September 1941, and 29 November 1941.

Bred and trained by S. J. Bryant of the Bridgewater, Somerset National Pigeon Service Group, NURP 38 BPC 6 made three flights from France including one made at the height of the war in September 1941. This was completed within 48 hours of the bird being dropped behind German lines.

Princess
Pigeon No. 42 WD 593
Date of Award: May 1946
Sent on special mission to Crete, this pigeon returned to her loft (RAF Alexandria) having travelled about 500 miles mostly over sea, with most valuable information. One of the finest performances in the war record of the Pigeon Service.

Another bird about whom very little is known, and a rare Dickin Medal connection with the eastern Mediterranean, Princess was based at RAF Alexandria. During the early years of the war the station was home to 228 Squadron, one of the first to employ Short Sunderland and Supermarine Stranraer flying boats. During both World Wars its pilots and crews were engaged in anti-submarine patrols, reconnaissance roles and air-sea rescue, and the likelihood is that at the start of her working life Princess was one of the birds routinely carried on missions.

Crete, the largest and most heavily populated Greek island, was an important target for German aggression and the base of the Greek Royal family after their escape from Athens. In May 1941 a major German airborne assault – Operation Mercury – heralded the start of the Battle of Crete. The Germans met with stiff resistance from the islanders and some 32,000 military personnel from British, Australian and New Zealand forces.

Initially the battle went in the defenders' favour. Thereafter a breakdown in communication, and a failure on the part of the Allied commanders fully to understand the threat of the first massed airborne invasion in military history, enabled the invaders to establish a foothold in the town of Maleme. With 750 glider troops, around 10,000 paratroops, 5,000 airlifted mountain troops standing by and 7,000 arriving by sea, the airstrip outside the town was soon secured, enabling reinforcements and heavy weapons to be flown in using nearly 500 aircraft. A mere seven of these were shot down, and within ten days the battle was all but over. Crete was in German hands and remained so until the surrender of the Axis powers in 1945.

Two squadrons of the RAF, Nos 30 and 33, were particularly badly hit during the invasion and there is a memorial to their dead on the island between Maleme and Tavronitis. Among those killed ahead of the Allies' collapse was the South African pilot Squadron Leader Marmaduke Pattle. The Commonwealth's leading air ace, with in excess of 40 kills to his credit, Pattle had twice been awarded the Distinguished Flying Cross before going down with three comrades in a flight of 12 Hawker Hurricanes. The battle also resulted in three servicemen being awarded the Victoria Cross, one going to a New Zealander who, hearing of his brother's death, single-handedly killed 33 Germans.

While victorious, the Germans sustained very heavy casualties, heavy enough for Hitler to rule out a similar operation taking place elsewhere at a future date. In part this was because the battle for Crete was one of the first opportunities Allied forces had to profit from the cracking of the Enigma codes, although to a degree this advantage was squandered by the decision not to bomb Cretan airfields on the understanding that the RAF would need them once the island was recaptured.

The cost to the defenders was also far heavier than anything suffered by the Germans, with around 4,000 killed and more than four times that number taken prisoner. It was one of the first actions where the Germans encountered significant resistance from civilians, and this continued despite the threat of reprisals. The Nazis' own records suggest they were eventually responsible for the execution of nearly 3,500 Cretan civilians and the massacre of another 1,000 or more, many during well-documented atrocities in the Amari Valley and against such villages as Kandanos and Kondomari.

While the credit for resistance rightly belongs to the local population, the people who paid by far the highest price, some outside assistance was rendered by the likes of John Pendlebury, an archaeologist and British intelligence representative. He successfully mobilised resistance ahead of the battle, while others active in the same arena included the writer Patrick Leigh Fermor, Tom Dunbabin and Xan Fielding, all three members of the Special Operations Executive.

It seems highly likely that the 'special mission' undertaken by Princess involved some kind of liaison between the SOE on the island and the Allied authorities in Alexandria – although again, with many confidential papers still unreleased, the nature of the mission and the message she carried remains unknown.

Rob
Collie
War Dog 471/322 Special Air Service
Date of Award: 22 January 1945
Took part in landings during North African Campaign with an Infantry unit and later served with a Special Air Unit in Italy as patrol and guard on small detachments lying-up in enemy territory. His presence with these parties saved many of them from discovery and subsequent capture or destruction. Rob made over 20 parachute descents.

Included in this chapter after serving with the special forces, Rob the dog's story also provides the starkest possible contrast with those of the often but undeservedly anonymous NPS Special Section pigeons.

Officially War Dog No. 471/332 Special Air Service, Rob was a characterful collie who earned his spurs in infantry landings during the North African campaign before joining a special air unit. As well as taking part in undercover operations in Italy, when he was engaged in patrol and guard duty on small detachments lying-up in enemy territory, Rob is said to have made more than 20 parachute jumps, many into enemy occupied territory, during the course of his training and the Allied push through Italy.

His presence on raiding and reconnaissance parties is reported to have saved several comrades from discovery and possible capture. It also made him something of a wartime celebrity, one of the first 'para-dogs', whose story and image rendered him irresistible to reporters and correspondents keen to inject some colour into their coverage of the war.

More recently it has been suggested the whole thing was a hoax – a 'shaggy dog story' is what the *Daily Telegraph* called it

– or that some aspects of Rob's life were deliberately exaggerated. With the combatants all now dead it is hard to verify the facts, although it seems extraordinary that an award so rarely given would be presented to an animal without the necessary checks being carried out. It must also be significant that he remains the only animal to be recommended for a Dickin Medal by the War Office and that during the course of his life he received another seven awards.

Rob's life began in Shropshire, where he became a strong-willed but a 'ordinary cattle collie' owned by a farming family called Bayne. Mostly black, with white legs and a distinctive eye patch on his white face, he was nearly four years old when he was sent on loan to the War Office and recruited into 2nd SAS. After training at Northaw, which he passed through in record time, Rob found himself posted overseas and in North Africa quickly proved himself adept at guard duties. (Memorably it was soon being said that 'Italian PoWs walked sideways past him and pilfering Arabs became honest men overnight.') SAS Quartermaster Major Burt was convinced the dog had greater talents, however, and consideration was given to training him as the canine equivalent of a Special Forces soldier – a resourceful individual able to put stealth, silence and strength to good purpose.

To test this out Rob is assumed to have been smuggled aboard an aeroplane and observed to see how he well he responded to the noise and motion. He must have been fine, because on a subsequent flight Rob bailed out wearing a borrowed US harness. Reportedly completely unfazed by this singular experience, the dog was then officially cleared for further training. He eventually completed 18 training jumps, on each occasion showing the willingness to be the first to jump if only his handler would let him.

Back in Shropshire the family received a note advising them that their pet was 'fit and well and doing a splendid job of work', one of his duties being to round up parachutists whose night vision was less good than his own. By this time Rob had moved with his unit to Italy, operating behind enemy lines ahead of the main Anglo-American force, which had invaded following the conquest of Tunisia and the surrender of Axis forces there in May 1943.

During this period Rob made two parachute jumps into occupied territory and possibly a third landing by sea although it is not possible to say where or when this might have taken place. All such actions were of course never anything but dangerous in the extreme, but it is worth noting that both of Rob's jumps took place following an order from Adolf Hitler himself that from this point all enemy parachutists were to be killed rather than rounded up and held with ordinary PoWs.

Unfortunately, as with many Special Forces operations, it is not possible even now to state with certainty the nature of the deed for which the award of a Dickin Medal was recommended, nor do the letters sent back to the Baynes family praising Rob seem to provide many clues. But one of the jumps the dog made into Italy was part of a bid to rescue Allied soldiers and airmen, and this might explain why, after the war, he made a number of appearances in London and the provinces at fund-raising events for the Returned Prisoners of War Fund.

It is also known that Rob had something of a lucky escape following his return to Britain, when the quarantine authorities refused to release him for further SAS duties until he had completed his six months in kennels. Unable to delay, his unit left without him, crossing Belgium and Holland before reaching Arnhem (see pages 46-50), where many of his erstwhile comrades died or sustained horrendous injuries.

Official recognition for Rob was not long in coming, the War Office citation stating unequivocally, 'there is no doubt that his presence with these [raiding] parties saved many of them from being discovered, and thereby from being captured and killed'. While it has since been said that elements of his story were made up, the Allied Forces Mascot Club was clearly happy to accept a recommendation from the very heart of the establishment. In February 1945 Rob was duly presented with his Dickin Medal by Major the Honourable William Philip Sidney, a veteran of the Italian campaign who was himself awarded the Victoria Cross for leading the defence at Anzio despite being seriously wounded.

Rob lived on until the age of 12, the Baynes family grateful to have him back although his training meant that in retirement he was reportedly much better at guarding the children than rounding up farm animals. Offered a place at the PDSA cemetery at Ilford (like all Dickin Medal recipients) in 1952 he was instead buried in Shropshire. His headstone records not just his three and a half years' service in Italy and North Africa but that he was 'a faithful friend and playmate' to the Baynes children, Heather and Basil. Following his death he was not replaced as a pet.

Rob made more than 20 parachute drops while serving with the
2nd Special Air Regiment in Italy

Chapter 9

Keeping the Peace

Since the establishment near London in 1942 of the first Army War Dogs school these intelligent and dependable animals have played an important part in maintaining law and order overseas. From mainland Europe during World War II through Palestine in the late 1940s and Bosnia-Herzegovina to Iraq and Afghanistan's Helmand Province, many thousands have been trained to work alongside peacekeepers, and have seen action in many different conflict zones.

The United Nations Charter gives the UN Security Council responsibility for the majority of such missions, the council authorising sometimes enormous and enduring peacekeeping initiatives involving the combined forces of NATO and member states. For the men and women on the ground who implement these initiatives the work is hard, dangerous and sometimes extremely prolonged. It is also highly complex as it can involve overseeing the orderly withdrawal of hostile forces over a wide area, the suppression of often very well-armed insurgencies and the maintenance of an agreed ceasefire.

More recently such missions have also begun to include the planning and gradual implementation of diplomatic and democratic processes. Taken with the inescapable fact that many such operations involve more peace enforcement than simple maintainence, the effect of this can be to extend the duration of the mission as well as putting UN and NATO troops in even greater danger. The experience of Iraq and Afghanistan, for example, has shown how so-called mopping-up operations can last longer, and actually prove deadlier, than the conflicts which preceded them.

Wherever they have been deployed, dogs have proved invaluable in such work, fulfilling a variety of crucial functions from guard duties to tracking. When used for mine clearance a well-trained animal can search up to 1,500 square metres a day. This represents a 300 per cent improvement over a human doing the job manually, and today an estimated 800 such animals are thought to be working in two dozen different countries alongside the armed forces and specialised non-governmental organisations.

As we have seen, such dogs provide an important additional service, bringing company, devotion and real companionship to their handlers and to the many servicemen and -women who have left pets at home as well as families. In a few well-documented examples, including those described in this chapter, the best of them have also shown genuinely selfless gallantry when finding themselves called to act in the most dangerous circumstances.

Punch
Boxer dog
Judy
Boxer bitch
Date of Awards: November 1946
These dogs saved the lives of two British Officers in Palestine by attacking an armed terrorist who was stealing upon them unawares and thus warning them of their danger. Punch sustained four bullet wounds and Judy a long graze down her back.

It is well known that the British played a substantial role in helping to establish the new state of Israel for the Jewish people, the 1917 Balfour Declaration stating unequivocally, 'His Majesty's Government view with favour the establishment in Palestine of a national home for the Jewish people, and will use their best endeavours to facilitate the achievement of this object.' Fine words are one thing, however, and the road towards securing this historic homeland for Holocaust survivors and Jews fleeing from elsewhere in Europe was to prove hard and dangerous to travel.

Nearly three decades on from Balfour, in the immediate post-war period, the state of Israel was still not established. British forces were present in considerable numbers but by no means welcome in Jerusalem and the surrounding territory, despite Britain's leading role in rolling back the Ottoman occupier in one world war, and defeating the Nazis in the next. With his firmly expressed sympathy for the Jewish struggle Churchill had been strongly behind the creation of a new state; but for a generation or more successive British governments had made conflicting and inconsistent commitments, and by 1946 Jewish patience was finally exhausted.

As the British authorities continued to enforce controversial limitations on Jews escaping Europe for Palestine, tension in the Middle East mounted and violent incidents frequently occurred. Already active in the 1930s, Zionist freedom fighters such as the Irgun and the Stern Gang now conducted their own campaigns against the British military and other targets hostile to their aims. The Arabs also had their own squabbles with the former imperial power, making this corner of the Middle East an explosive place. Against this background the first PDSA Dickin Medals to be awarded for an action in peacetime, or perhaps one should say the first following the defeat of the Axis powers, went to two Boxer dogs.

Called Punch and Judy, the siblings belonged to a couple of senior British army officers who shared quarters in Jerusalem: Lieutenant Colonel A. H. K. Campbell, a deputy judge advocate of the Jerusalem Military Court, and Lieutenant Colonel Hugh G. G. Niven of the 1st Battalion Royal Berkshire Regiment, in Palestine as adjutant general.

Campbell's appointment was potentially hazardous as on more than one occasion death sentences were passed in the court and carried out on individuals since considered within Israel to be national heroes. By July 1946, with tensions already running high, things were threatening to come to a head and on the 22nd of that month the Irgun attack on Jerusalem's King David Hotel led to 91 deaths. Churchill, typically, managed to counter his natural sense of outrage by reflecting on Britain's shilly-shallying over the issue since 1917, but the carnage was awful.

On the evening of 5 August 1946 the threat to British personnel was again demonstrated when the two officers were relaxing at home. It was a quiet night and a hot one, so the door to the house had been left open to admit some fresh air. When one of the men moved towards the doorway at approximately 22.30 both dogs suddenly leapt up, running towards it and then out into the pitch black barking frantically. At once a burst of sub-machine gun fire echoed round the garden, followed by a sharp yelp from one of the dogs. The assailant quickly disappeared into the night, but can be assumed to have borne a grudge against one or both men, whom he intended to kill.

When the police arrived it did not take long to locate the dogs. Following a trail of blood they found Judy, who was standing over the badly injured Punch. Both dogs were covered in blood, and a quick examination showed Punch had been hit a number of times. A superintendent was immediately summoned from the PDSA dispensary in Jerusalem – until the 1970s the charity was active in eight African and Middle Eastern countries – and discovered that Colonel Niven's dog had been hit no fewer than four times. One bullet had struck him below one eye, another in the left shoulder, and a third in the groin. A fourth bullet had badly seared the top of Punch's skull, and he was estimated to have lost approximately three quarters of a pint of blood.

Fortunately the prompt attention the dog received, and his general fitness, meant the prognosis looked good. Judy had a long graze across her back but most of the blood on her coat had clearly come from her brother. Happily both made a full recovery, and although a further five spent rounds were found in the compound surrounding the house the assassin was not caught nor his identity ever established.

Shortly after being declared fit the dogs were repatriated to England and at the inaugural Royal Tournament held at Olympia in west London the following year the pair were presented with Dickin Medals.

Since then the medals have become separated. When a London auctioneer offered for sale one clearly marked 'Judy, Army H.Q. Palestine 5-8-46 AFMC.1195 No. 44' in May 2011, the corresponding medal for her brother did not form part of the lot although the citation offered at the same time named both dogs. Complete with its ring suspension and described in the catalogue as 'very fine and better', Judy's medal was nevertheless sold for £7,200.

Lucky
German shepherd
RAF No. 3610 AD
Royal Air Force Police anti-terrorist tracker dog
Date of Award: 6 February 2007 (posthumous)
For the outstanding gallantry and devotion to duty of the RAF

Police anti-terrorist tracker dog team, comprising Bobbie, Jasper, Lassie and Lucky, while attached to the Civil Police and several British Army regiments including the Coldstream Guards, 2nd Battalion Royal Scots Guards and the Gurkhas during the Malaya Campaign. Bobbie, Jasper, Lassie and Lucky displayed exceptional determination and life-saving skills during the 1949–52 Malaya Campaign. The dogs and their handlers were an exceptional team, capable of tracking and locating the enemy by scent despite unrelenting heat and an almost impregnable jungle. Sadly, three of the dogs lost their lives in the line of duty: only Lucky survived to the end of the conflict.

In February 2007 at London's Imperial War Museum, when Lance Corporal Karen Yardley RAVC accepted on her dog Sadie's behalf a Dickin Medal from HRH the Princess Alexandra (see page 68), another award was given. This was a rare post-humous medal, awarded to the dog Lucky on behalf of all four of the above-named dogs, who saw service in Malaya with the Royal Air Force Police 1949–52.

Happily by now long retired, Corporal Bevel Austin Stapleton – Bev to his comrades – was on hand to accept the medal more than half a century after stepping down as the popular German shepherd's RAFP handler. Air Dog 3610 had been trained as a specialist tracker, her job to patrol deep into jungle territory where the RAFP were helping to find and capture communist insurgents. Their work formed part of what the colonial authorities in London preferred to call the Malayan Emergency, although it can now be seen as a national war of liberation.

However described it was very much a guerilla war, something which in part may explain why such a lethal 12-year campaign (it cost upwards of 12,000 lives) has to a great degree been eclipsed in the British public's memory by the militarily more conventional Cold War struggle which was taking place in Korea over much of the same period.

The Emergency saw some 40,000 British and Commonwealth troops pitched against a determined but much smaller force of approximately 8,000 communists. These were chiefly ethnic Chinese rather than Malays – a group long established in the area but still denied many legal rights. They targeted mineral extraction and industrial operations such as tin mines and rubber plantations in order to drive out their despised colonial overlords.

Following moves to outlaw communist organisations in 1948 the insurgents retreated to rural areas before eventually disappearing into the jungle. Initially at least they were largely successful, in part because many of them had been trained in this type of fighting by the British during the war in order to defeat the Japanese. Some of the groups were well armed too, having failed to turn in their British-supplied weapons in 1945.

Those British forces already in the country needed to be supplemented, and before long the strength included Gurkhas, Royal Marines, men from the King's African Rifles and the Special Air Service, which had been newly re-formed to provide specialised reconnaissance, raiding and counter-insurgency patrols. The murder of the British High Commissioner in October 1951 brought yet more heat into an already dangerous situation, but even before this the men and dogs of the Royal Air Force Police were daily engaged in tracking and capturing their targets and had soon notched up many successes.

Two of Lucky's companions were to be accidentally electrocuted while crossing a waterway, but together the four are known to have been instrumental in the capture of many hundreds of enemy combatants, and the communist insurgency was eventually neutralised. Like much about this little-known chapter in

British colonial history, details are still vague, although one of those reported to have been captured by Lucky and her companion was was Lang Jan-Sang. A man described by the *Daily Mail* as a 'murderous communist gang leader', he was known to have terrorised and murdered many Malay villagers.

Today little more is known than that, but the RAF Police continue to play an important role in international peacekeeping. At the time of writing its men and women are employed countering the threat from IEDs in Afghanistan and working with Afghan National Police liaison teams. In such work they still rely on dogs, predominantly German shepherds for 'attack' roles with Labradors and spaniels employed to locate drugs and explosives.

Sam
German shepherd
Royal Army Veterinary Corps
Date of Award: 14 January 2003
For outstanding gallantry in April 1998 while assigned to the Royal Canadian Regiment in Drvar during the conflict in Bosnia-Herzegovina. On two documented occasions Sam displayed great courage and devotion to duty. On 18 April Sam successfully brought down an armed man threatening the lives of civilians and Service personnel. On 24 April, while guarding a compound harbouring Serbian refugees, Sam's determined approach held off rioters until reinforcements arrived. This dog's true valour saved the lives of many servicemen and civilians during this time of human conflict.

One of the many largely unsung heroes of the bloody break-up of the former Yugoslavia, Sam was a German shepherd trained by the Royal Army Veterinary Corps for guard and patrol duties in Bosnia-Herzegovina in the late 1990s.

The country had unilaterally declared itself sovereign and then independent on 3 March 1992, a move which led to an explosion of inter-communal violence in an area which had long been home to three distinct ethnic groups. This rapidly spiralled, leading to accusations of ethnic cleansing, mass murder and even genocide. By 1995 NATO was conducting a sustained air campaign, Operation Deliberate Force, deploying 400 aircraft, and using more than 5,000 ground personnel to protect so-called safe areas from Serb attacks and to enforce an internationally agreed no-fly zone.

While the outcome can scarcely be called decisive, the NATO air strikes were instrumental in bringing all parties to the negotiating table, and following the Dayton Peace Agreement, signed in November 1995, peacekeepers were deployed to the area. The initial implementation force (IFOR) was followed by SFOR, charged with stabilisation. SFOR depended on personnel from more than three dozen countries, NATO and non-NATO members. Attached to the 1st Battalion, Royal Canadian Regiment, Sam and his handler Corporal Iain Carnegie formed part of the NATO contingent charged with the complex and dangerous task of enforcing peace rather than just maintaining it.

On 18 April 1998 the pair were patrolling the western town of Drvar, a town historically predominantly Serb but by this time largely Croat following a campaign to move Croats into homes which had previously been owned and occupied by Serbs. With the latter returning home in numbers, riots and murders became commonplace with displaced Serbs finding themselves shut out of their former homes and business premises or the same buildings looted and burned out.

It was against this incendiary background that Sam twice performed acts of outstanding courage and devotion to duty. In the first of these he successfully identified and brought down an armed man who was endangering the lives of local people and SFOR personnel. After firing on a patrol, the man was observed running into a bar. Sam followed him in and disabled him, enabling his handler to confiscate a handgun and place him under arrest. According to his handler, Sam 'performed brilliantly, just like a training exercise'.

Six days later, while tasked with guarding a compound harbouring returning Serbs, the pair were instrumental in holding off a large group of rioting Croats. The rioters, about 50 of them, were armed with clubs, but undaunted by a hail of missiles and broken bottles, Sam stood his ground until reinforcements arrived from the Royal Canadian Regiment. Subsequently promoted to sergeant, Carnegie later told a reporter from the *Daily Telegraph*, 'by threatening them with pistols and dogs we forced our way into the compound. We kept the rioters at bay until reinforcements arrived.' Sam's valour, he said, undoubtedly saved the lives of many servicemen and civilians. 'I could never have attempted to carry out my duties without him.'

Sam retired two years later, aged ten, but sadly died shortly afterwards. His death was ascribed to natural causes. It was left to Sergeant Carnegie to accept the medal on his behalf at a special ceremony held at the Army Medical Directorate (Sandhurst), something he described as a great honour. Recognising, in the words of the PDSA's then chairman Major Roy Trustram Eve, that 'from the accounts we received detailing Sam's gallantry during his tour in Bosnia there is no doubt that this dog deserves the highest recognition' it was the first Dickin Medal to be awarded to an army dog in nearly 60 years.

Chapter 10

Search and Rescue: the Blitz

Today the use of dogs to locate people lost beneath the rubble of ruined buildings is standard practice; indeed it is such a logical extension of other search-and-rescue techniques employed in time of war and after natural disasters that it is hard to appreciate that its beginnings in the Britain of the 1940s were incidental if not entirely accidental.

Elsewhere search dogs had already proved their worth, for example in the western Alps, where there is documentary evidence from as early as 1707 of large solidly built dogs being kept for this purpose. Their keepers were monks in a hospice on the sometimes treacherous Great St Bernard Pass between Switzerland and Italy. During the Great War other breeds were trained by the Red Cross to find injured soldiers on the battle-fields of the Western Front.

On the Home Front however the requirement for something similar became apparent only with the Blitz, when the sustained bombing of London and other major cities from September 1940 brought the reality of war into people's lives. Causing massive physical damage as well as widespread disruption and the deaths of more than 40,000 civilians, the German campaign failed to have the desired impact on public morale, but in London alone more than a million houses were damaged or destroyed. While not every raid produced casualties, the authorities were in danger of being swamped by calls for help from residents convinced that a friend or family member was buried somewhere in the rubble.

Against this background the appearance of Rip was serendipitous to say the least. Together with Tipperary Beauty, one of the real search-dog pioneers, and as such one of the more famous faces of the PDSA Dickin Medal, this scruffy underfed East End stray was taken in by a kindly Air Raid Precautions (ARP) warden based at Poplar. Instinctively good at finding Blitz victims, his example – which is detailed below – was in large part responsible for the rapid adoption of official sniffer dogs, scores of which were trained to trace casualties and which between them saved many hundreds of lives.

Rip
Mongrel
Stray picked up by Civil Defence squad at Poplar, London E14
Date of Award: July 1945
For locating many air-raid victims during the Blitz of 1940.

Typically the stories told about this plucky little East End waif describe how he was adopted by Mr E. King, an ARP warden

Rip with handler Mr King

based at Post B132 in Southill Street between Poplar's Langdon Park and the East India Dock Road. A more accurate description of the start of the close relationship which developed between the two and lasted for more than five years might be that the dog adopted the man. Mr King always claimed to have found him 'homeless and hungry after a heavy raid in September 1940. I did not know him and I thought that after a feed he would have gone away. But he attached himself to me.'

King and his colleagues took Rip on as a sort of unofficial post mascot, and it was soon apparent that with his keen sense of smell, sense of adventure and intrepid terrier-like nature the little mongrel was able to offer more than a little casual companionship during the chilly autumn nights. Before long he was accompanying Warden King on his nightly rounds of the street shelters, picking up the odd titbit from locals always happy to see a familiar face in the gloom of the blackout.

Situated close to the docks, Post B132 had what Warden King described as 'many bad incidents, and Rip soon proved his worth. He was very valuable in helping us to locate persons trapped in the debris and during the alerts, heavy gunfire and incendiary raids Rip was always out on duty – never in the way but always eager to do his bit.'

As well as showing unfailing enthusiasm, Rip had a real talent for the job and far from needing training demonstrated time and again not only that he understood what was required but knew the best way to achieve it. Braving smoke, fire, explosions from delayed-action fuses, falling masonry and the inevitable hazards of clambering over charred and unstable ruins, what other dogs were later taught through weeks of intensive specialist training Rip knew intuitively.

Because of this all Rip's training, insisted King, 'was gained the hard way. He had over five years' active service to his credit, and when I came across Rip sniffing around on the job I always knew that there was someone trapped in the ruins.' Rip's sensitive nose, the metronomic beat of his short stubby tail and those little paws pushing away at bricks and masonry were often the first sign that somebody was down there and needed help. (His probably quite random ancestry was never established, but the similarity between Rip and a Jack Russell after a rabbit was noted on more than one occasion.)

The area around the docks was a favourite destination for the Luftwaffe and the most heavily bombed civilian target of the war. With Germany attempting to paralyse the commercial life of the capital by destroying its docks, wharves and warehouses, the people of east London found themselves in the direct line of fire. Within two months of the Blitz starting, around 40 per cent of houses in Stepney had been damaged, and in the borough of West Ham nearly a third of the houses had been actually destroyed. Rip's area similarly took an exceptionally heavy pounding, putting extraordinary pressure on the local Civil Defence services, and in all he is known to have saved more than a hundred lives.

Even so Rip was far more than a rescue dog. Besides demonstrating the important role that dogs could play on the Home Front, his cheerful spirit and lively personality was a great boon to those who met him on his nightly rounds. As Jilly Cooper noted in her book *Animals in War*, 'how welcome to the victims must have been the first sounds of those scrabbling paws and shrill terrier yaps, and the first sight of the grinning Tommy Brock face with its merry friendly eyes'.

In 1945, two years after the institution of the Dickin Medal, Rip was presented with one of his own, which he wore on a daily basis. Sadly, his age always uncertain, he was to survive the war by little more than a year. In 1946 he visibly slowed and was diagnosed with oedema or dropsy – an abnormal build-up of fluid in cavities beneath the skin – and in the autumn of the same year Rip passed away. On 15 October Rip DM became the first of a dozen medal recipients to be laid to rest at the Ilford PDSA Animal Cemetery, Essex.

Rip's story continues to resonate, however, doubtless given added appeal by his street-urchin character and implacable spirit. In April 2009 in London the medal and coin dealers Spink announced they would be auctioning Rip's Dickin Medal, which was expected to fetch between £8,000 and £10,000. Five years previously the same company had sold the medal awarded to Commando (see page 129), a pigeon which saw service with the Special Operations Executive, for £9,200. This time considerable interest in the room and by telephone resulted in an anonymous bidder eventually paying an astonishing £24,250 for a real piece of London's wartime history.

Beauty
Wire-haired terrier
PDSA rescue squad serving with Civil Defence
Date of Award: 12 January 1945
For being the pioneer dog in locating buried air-raid victims while serving with a PDSA Rescue Squad.

A popular mascot of one of the wartime PDSA rescue squads, Beauty was another early pioneer in the field of search and rescue, a wire-haired terrier who like Rip took it upon herself to provide a useful service to members of her squad. This was tasked with rescuing and caring for animals who had lost their homes – and not infrequently their owners – in the destruction which rained down on London from the night skies.

At the outbreak of hostilities PDSA converted a number of its mobile dispensaries and animal ambulances into rescue vehicles and, posted at strategic points up and down the country, the rescue squads worked under the auspices of the National ARP for Animals Committee. In 1939 London alone was home to some 400,000 dogs and an estimated 1.5 million cats, many tens of thousands of which were destroyed by owners fearful of the coming war. The rescue squads, even so, are known to have aided and treated more than 256,000 domestic pets and other animals injured by fire and debris resulting from enemy action.

Working closely with Civil Defence personnel, squad members were charged with searching shattered and burned-out buildings, combing the ruins and other areas where unexploded ordnance required the population to be evacuated. Giving first aid to any injured animals they also made longer-term arrangements for the care of the cats and dogs which emerged from the wreckage following air raids.

The work might have been left to ARP personnel, but with 25,000 bombs falling in and around the docks the latter were already heavily overworked. Dealing with the unfolding human tragedy they also faced the dangers consequent upon thousands of buildings being rendered unsafe and unstable. Viewed against this background, the notion of rescuing what to some are mere pets may seem a small concern, but both during and after the war the

Civil Defence authorities expressed their gratitude to the charity's rescue squads and recognised their considerable contribution.

Besides the obvious moral worth of reducing suffering among animals, the prospect of London in ruins and crawling with tens of thousands of starving, sometimes horrifically injured, ownerless and increasingly desperate cats and dogs was a worrying one. The rescue of animals was also of immeasurable worth when their owners could be identified. Particularly in those far-from-rare cases when a family had lost literally everything else it possessed, the return of a much-loved pet could provide a huge boost to their morale and keep them battling on.

Tipperary Beauty – often just Beauty – belonged to Bill Barnet, a bespectacled PDSA superintendent assigned to one of the rescue squads based in east London. One evening in 1940, when she was barely a year old, Beauty was observed pawing at some rubble a little way from where Barnet and his team were working. Trusting the little dog's instincts as her digging became faster and more frantic, and struck by her determination, Barnet and a couple of colleagues moved across and started to excavate. It was hard work, but a few minutes' labour found Beauty's quarry: a terrified cat trapped beneath a kitchen table.

The cat, injured but alive, was to be the first of 63 rescues attributed to Beauty and Bill Barnet, and rarely if ever did her intuition let her down. Like the similarly enthusiastic mongrel Rip, her efforts were always unofficial but nevertheless deeply appreciated, and when it became apparent that she was sustaining injuries pawing at the jagged fragments of London's shattered streets she was presented with two pairs of leather bootees, specially made to protect the little dog's feet.

Appreciation also came in the form of one of the charity's prestigious Pioneer Medals – an award generally reserved for human beings – and a smart silver-mounted collar presented to Beauty by

Alderman C. Beaumont Teare in his role as deputy mayor of Hendon. To this must be added a silver medal 'for Services Rendered' from the mayor of Salford in Lancashire together with the Freedom of Holland Park, which in theory at least gave her unrestricted access to the park 'and all the trees therein'.

Beauty's Dickin Medal had to wait a short while longer, however, but on 12 January 1945 at a ceremony presided over by the polar explorer Admiral of the Fleet Sir Edward Evans KCB DSO, 1st Baron Mountevans, her gallantry and splendid service were formally recognised by the organisation she had served so well.

Leaving London for a well-earned retirement in the north, Beauty lived for another five years, passing away peacefully on 17 October 1950. She joined Rip at the cemetery at Ilford, her Dickin Medal being returned to PDSA for safekeeping. Together with her silver collar and silver medal, this went on display as part of the Imperial War Museum's The Animals' War exhibition in 2006.

Jet (of Iada)
German shepherd
Ministry of Aircraft Production (serving with Civil Defence)
Date of Award: 12 January 1945
For being responsible for the rescue of persons trapped under blitzed buildings while serving with the Civil Defence Services of London.

Following the somewhat belated recognition by the Civil Defence authorities that dogs could perform a valuable role in urban search and rescue it was perhaps inevitable that once the process was formalised new recruits would not be selected from among the scruffy likes of Rip and Beauty.

Jet of Iada and her companion Crumstone Irma were therefore very much of the new generation, two handsome German shepherds whose highfalutin monikers betrayed a certain measure of breeding and pedigree.

Jet had already started training before being posted to London. Leaving Liverpool and the home of well-known dog breeder Mrs Hilda Babcock Cleaver at the age of nine months, the black Alsatian and his four siblings were sent to Gloucestershire for a trial at the new Ministry of Aircraft Production Guard Dog School.

Established in 1942 by Great War veteran Lieutenant Colonel F. Y. Baldwin at Woodfold near Tewkesbury, the school existed primarily to train dogs and their handlers in anti-sabotage and patrol work, the idea being that with more effective dogs hundreds of personnel could be released from guard duty to undertake more skilled tasks. Having seen for himself many *Deutsche Schäferhunde* in action during his time in the trenches, Baldwin was convinced that German shepherds' keen sense of smell, their speed, endurance, aggression and above all courage could be put to good use again – only this time working for rather than against HM Forces.

His instincts proved correct, and before long dog patrols were being used to boost the perimeter security of a growing number of military factories, airfields and equipment stores against sabotage, espionage and straightforward theft. At the same time, continued attacks, by aircraft and increasingly towards the end of the war by V-1 and V-2 rockets, meant that Civil Defence personnel in London and other major cities were always stretched. By 1944 several years' experience of searching ruined buildings had resulted in an impressive record of success when it came to locating the dead and injured after every raid. Manpower could only reach so far, however, and even skilled searchers were forced to rely on sight and experience rather than the sort of instinct shown by Rip and Beauty. To rectify this, the decision was belatedly taken to train some of these more specialist dogs in search-and-rescue techniques.

Initially 14 were dispatched to London for this purpose, and with five of them subsequently being awarded the Dickin Medal it was perhaps scarcely necessary for the authorities – as eventually they did – to admit that the initiative might more sensibly have been taken earlier in the war. Among the 14 was Jet of Iada, who after a spell in Northern Ireland with the American Army Air Force travelled up to the capital in the back of a truck with his handler, RAF Corporal C. Wardle in September 1944.

Reportedly a poor traveller and disconcerted by the journey, Jet nevertheless hit the ground running and within a couple of hours of his arrival was taken from his new home at Civil Defence Depot 1 at Cranmer Court in Chelsea to an incident at Edmonton.

Jet immediately went to the correct spot, and a casualty was dug out from the wreckage and treated for his injuries. Jet's performance should have surprised no one. During his training in anti-sabotage work he had managed to locate a 'sniper' – in reality one of his trainers – who had concealed himself more than a dozen feet underground. Thereafter it was accepted that he had an extraordinarily keen sense of smell. In London, amid the fire, smoke and chaos which accompanied every attack (for all such dogs burned paws were a common occupational hazard) Jet is believed to have been called out every night until the raids ceased, but in all that time was never known to give his handler a wrong indication of where a casualty might be found.

Of course not infrequently Jet and his companions would uncover bodies rather than the merely wounded, but this too must be looked upon as a very valuable service, both to the families of the bereaved and in terms of public health and safety. Of the 125 individuals located by Jet between his arrival in London and VE Day an estimated 50 were pulled from the ground alive. Such a tally does much to explain the eventual awarding of a Dickin Medal, although one incident more than any other may have brought this outstanding dog to the attention of a wider audience.

In October 1944 an hotel close to Jet's barracks in Chelsea received a direct hit from an enemy bomb. A number of people were rescued from the smoking ruins and after some time the search-and-rescue team were preparing to withdraw when Jet's demeanour led Corporal Wardle to suspect that they still had some more work to do. Jet seemed to be indicating that someone was trapped above ground, his agitated manner an indication that the person was still alive as in cases where the dog had located a body he would sit calmly while the team excavated around him.

The search was renewed, still to no avail, yet the dog refused to stand down. Finally a longer ladder was brought in, and picking their way carefully through the ruins to what had been the top storey of the hotel, the rescuers eventually came to a ledge on which they found a woman in her mid-60s. Exhausted, covered in dust and debris, but still clinging on, she was to make a full recovery.

By this time Jet had been on duty for nearly 12 hours, and according to many – including Mrs Lilias Ward, Mrs Babcock Cleaver's daughter – it was more for this impressive act of dedication and tenacity than any other that Jet was subsequently nominated for the Dickin Medal. Certainly the story made him something of a celebrity, and Jet was invited to take part in the official London Victory Parade on 8 June 1945 in Hyde Park attended by the Royal Family, Winston Churchill and his successor as prime minister, Clement Attlee.

Following the celebrations and the official standing-down of the Civil Defence Services two days later, Jet returned to his home city. After his sadly premature death from heart and kidney disease in October 1948, *The Times* reported that the seven-year-old dog was to be buried in Liverpool's Calderstones Park. Close by a memorial was erected to him after an approach from Mrs Babcock Cleaver to the city council, an unusual inscribed sundial on a fluted column. Unfortunately, this was subsequently stolen but it was replaced by a new monument by the sculptor Pablo Grassi in 2003. Another memorial is displayed in the city's Mansion House.

According to Mrs Ward, 'The main thing my mother wanted was for the story of the contribution made to the war effort by individuals and dogs as well, to be told to children, and for them to know the good things that dogs can do to help us.'

Jet

Crumstone Irma
German shepherd
Ministry of Aircraft Production (serving with Civil Defence)
Date of Award: 12 January 1945
For being responsible for the rescue of persons trapped under blitzed buildings while serving with the Civil Defences of London.

*

Recruited at the same time as Jet of Iada, Crumstone Irma was another well-bred hound. Irma came from the Goring-on-Thames kennels of Mrs Margaret Griffin, later awarded the British Empire Medal for her work as chief trainer at the Ministry of Aircraft Production Guard Dog School and for accompanying her own trainees on operations.

Recognised among dog breeders for their apparently exceptional intelligence and an impressive devotion to duty, Mrs Griffin's Crumstone line was descended from a dog she obtained in New Zealand. A number of them saw action in the 1940s, and indeed before being taken on by the ministry Irma and another Crumstone dog called Storm were used as messengers by the Leatherhead ARP. Trained to cover the more than three and a half miles from an ARP post to the Surrey Report Centre in the event of the telephone lines coming down, Storm once covered the distance in a couple of seconds under 14 minutes.

After being retrained at the MAP school, specifically in urban search-and-rescue techniques, Irma was paired with a dog called Psyche, the two of them going on to chalk up an astonishing tally of 233 rescues. From the start both displayed an unerring knack for locating victims, Mrs Griffin's meticulously kept diary (now in the possession of the MOD) and a letter to the Allied Forces Mascot Club in March 1945 referring to a typical incident involving the two dogs on an operation in London. After being called out to an incident in which people were still missing, 'Irma and Psyche together suddenly ran to a point in the debris. Beneath this rubble we found a collapsed floor. A woman was trapped there between two floors. She had been there over nine hours and was still conscious. We got her out and, after examination, the doctor said she had a good chance of recovery.'

Although the woman's child had sadly not survived, such a quick find was clearly remarkable in the circumstances, Mrs Griffin noting in the letter that the collapsed floors were entirely obscured by a mound of rubble so that the discovery of the woman was completely unexpected. Time and again, however, often when the assumption was that all had been lost, Psyche and Irma demonstrated their ability to locate live casualties – animals as well as humans Mrs Griffin would describe such occasions in her characteristically down-to-earth fashion as 'hours of work well spent' while always looking forward to the day when 'the bells of peace will be ringing out'.

Irma in particular seemed to have a nose for live victims, and she had a special bark when locating someone she somehow knew to be alive. On at least one occasion an apparently lifeless corpse was pulled from a building, but instead of licking its hand or face, as Irma often did when the discovery came too late, she continued barking until, after a minute or two, the victim slowly recovered consciousness. On another she refused to leave a scene for a full two days, at the conclusion of which two young girls were found in the ruins.

Yet another remarkable rescue took place in Chingford in February 1945, following a V-2 attack from a battery situated near the Hague. Striking in the early hours, the rocket destroyed several houses and badly damaged a number of others, and with a number of fatalities already confirmed Mrs Griffin and her dogs were sent for. Mrs Griffin's diary entry for the day describes a 'nasty mess. Rocket had gone right through one house. Gas was very bad up here, about 14 [feet] or a little more above ground level.' Quartering the scene with her typical speed and efficiency, Irma soon detected something in the rubble and silence was called for so that the rescuers could home in on any sounds from down below.

After 20 minutes searching and digging a baby was heard together with faint sounds believed to come from its mother. It turned out that three members of the Raven family were trapped in the ruins of their house beneath a Morrison Shelter – a type of reinforced kitchen table – and after two hours determined digging the rescuers were able to pull out a baby boy and his elder brother. Their mother had unfortunately died of asphyxiation at some point between Irma locating the family and the rubble being cleared away, one of four dead and 45 injured in the attack.

For Mrs Griffin it was one of scores of similar rescues, each one described at length, and happily both boys made a complete recovery. In 1950 they were reunited with Irma and her handler after being taken by their father to Earls Court for the annual Crufts Show. The press were on hand to record the event, the baby, Paul Raven, later telling the BBC, 'We all would have lost our lives had it not been for Irma and Psyche.'

By this time Irma had been something of a search-and-rescue celebrity for a number of years, having for example been chosen to march alongside Jet of Iada in the 1945 London Victory Parade. Following a tremendous fly-past over the Mall by no fewer than 35 squadrons of air force and naval aircraft, Irma and Mrs Griffin were presented to King George VI and Queen Elizabeth in Hyde Park. A photograph of their meeting shows a look of real admiration and affection on the face of Her Majesty, who is pictured looking down at the dog while her trainer and handler describes Irma's many unique achievements.

Irma licks the casualty she has found

Thorn
German shepherd
Ministry of Aircraft Production (serving with Civil Defence)
Date of Award: 2 March 1945
For locating air-raid casualties in spite of thick smoke in a burning building.

Yet another descendant of Echo, the splendid animal brought back from New Zealand by MAP Guard Dog School head trainer Margaret Griffin, Thorn may have scored fewer finds than Jet and Irma but nevertheless distinguished himself by his extraordinary courage. This manifested itself in his ability to battle on in the face of fire, and to overcome or at least disregard the aversion to smoke and flames that is natural to the vast majority of species. On numberless occasions he performed his duties at great personal danger to himself and his handler.

By June 1944 and D-Day, some two years after the establishment of the school, an estimated 7,000 dogs had been recruited and trained for a wide variety of tasks. These ranged from simple guard duties to carrying messages, and from sniffing out mines to locating victims – alive and dead – beneath collapsed buildings. The dreadful impact of Germany's V-1 and V-2 weapons made the latter skill all the more vital, the pilotless bombs arriving too late to turn the tide of the Allies' victory but nevertheless causing destruction on a massive scale across London and other cities.

The British-based *New Yorker* columnist Mollie Panter-Downes (1906–97) described how 'for Londoners there are no longer such things as good nights; there are only bad nights, worse nights and better nights [as] the *Blitzkrieg* continues to be directed against such military objectives as the tired shopgirl, the red-eyed clerk, and the thousands of dazed and weary families'. It is then little wonder that both the George Cross and George Medal have their origins at this time, created by the King specifically to acknowledge the heroism and bravery of non-military personnel dealing with the Blitz and its appalling aftermath. Fittingly the first of the new medals went to the men who saved St Paul's Cathedral from a massive unexploded bomb, an 800-pounder which was carefully excavated and removed to Hackney Marshes, where its controlled detonation created a 100-foot-wide crater.

With more than 9,250 V-1s or 'doodlebugs' launched against British targets and a further 1,115 V-2s – the vast majority of the latter targeted on London – death genuinely stalked the capital's streets 24 hours a day. At their peak an average of 155 were fired each day, and with thousands of houses damaged or destroyed the assaults continued until military advances on the continent enabled Allied forces to capture and disable the launch sites. Among the buildings which fell victim to the new weapons in the meantime were the Guards' Chapel at Wellington Barracks (killing 119 and injuring 102, some of whom subsequently died), the venerable London Library in St James's Square, St Thomas' Hospital, Selfridges, Sloane Court in Chelsea, and an animal health institute in south London. When Smithfield meat market was hit, 115 died, and several of the market workers were trapped in the cold storage vaults for a number of hours.

The worst incident of all, however, occurred when a branch of Woolworths in New Cross High Street was hit by a V-2 around lunchtime on 25 November 1944. The blast from its enormous 1,870-pound payload and falling masonry killed 168 and seriously injured more than 120 others. Despite around 1,000 men working for 48 hours on the south London site, eleven bodies were never found, including two babies sharing a pram.

In the face of such destruction a dog's most obvious advantage over human search-and-rescue personnel is of course its superior sense of smell. This is true even without specific training of the sort carried out by Mrs Griffin and her colleagues. That said, even now it is not well understood what it is that dogs detect. It could be skin rafts (scent-carrying cells that we shed at the rate of many thousands a day) or evaporated perspiration or respiratory gases – or of course, in the case of the deceased, gases released by the process of decomposition.

In Thorn's case the mystery is deeper still, however. Not simply because of his apparent willingness to rush fearlessly into wreckage – as we have seen many other dogs displayed this same attribute – but because time and again Thorn refused to be deterred by fire and smoke. Once in position he also appeared somehow to be able to detect minute traces of human scent beneath the choking and sometimes toxic odours of a burning street or factory.

In such a situation the air will be carrying a huge variety of different odours, most of which run together to confuse the average human, who, blessed with an estimated five million odour-sensing cells in his nose, is simply not well enough equipped to distinguish between the different scents. Canine species typically have around 220 million such cells, however, meaning they can discriminate even where one smell appears to us to overpower all others. This and their ability to 'taste' scents means they are able not just to detect a specific smell but to trace it to its source, even when the original source is no longer present.

None of which, of course, even begins to explain Thorn's ability to overcome the dread of fire which is innate in most if not all species, wild and domesticated. In the final analysis it was that which enabled him to go in where others quite literally feared to tread, and which led to the award of a Dickin Medal in the spring of 1945.

The official recommendation for the award came in a letter to the Mascot Club from Sir Edward Warner DSO, MC, which described perfectly the dog's courage and ability on an occasion which eventually led to the dog's handler being awarded the British Empire Medal. Sir Edward wrote how 'we then went to the houses which were on fire. Thorn went slowly step by step into the thickest smoke. He repeatedly flinched but was encouraged forward until eventually he reached a spot approximately over the seat of the fire and gave positive indication there. Casualties were subsequently recovered from this point.' In Sir Edward's opinion, as senior regional officer for London Civil Defence from 1942 until the war's conclusion, 'the work of Thorn at this spot was the best I have yet seen from any Rescue Dog.'

Curiously there was one thing which spooked Thorn. In 2006 Mrs Babcock Cleaver's son William recalled how the dog had been expected to take part in the aforementioned Victory celebrations in Hyde Park but had to be withdrawn. For a dog noted for his courage, and with performance as part of his pedigree – another of his forebears was rumoured to be

Hollywood's first canine star Rin Tin Tin – perhaps he was just being modest rather than shy.

Rex
German shepherd
Ministry of Aircraft Production (serving with Civil Defence)
Date of Award: April 1945
For outstanding good work in the location of casualties in burning buildings. Undaunted by smouldering debris, thick smoke, intense heat and jets of water from fire hoses, this dog displayed uncanny intelligence and outstanding determination in his efforts to follow up any scent which led him to a trapped casualty.

Modest or not, a number of decorated search-and-rescue dogs found themselves canine celebrities after the war, something that made them invaluable when it came to raising funds for the cash-strapped PDSA. Public appearances were regularly organised for this purpose, and often out of the crowd an individual would appear with a story to tell relating to the dog being introduced to the public that day.

One such occasion recalled by Mrs Babcock Cleaver's son William was a visit to the Tower of London by Jet of Iada. 'On their way a woman dashed from one side of the road to the other, oblivious of traffic and pedestrians, and threw her arms around his neck.' With tears streaming down her face but clearly delighted to see the dog and crying out, 'It's Jet, it's our Jet – I know it is!' the woman then emptied the contents of her purse into the collecting tin. Others may have been quieter and less demonstrative but their feelings were no less heartfelt. On another occasion in Birmingham a man came pushing through the crowd, put a pound note into the handler's hand and while patting Jet on the head murmured, 'Jet saved my life,' before disappearing back into the crowd.

Credited with saving 65 lives, the dog Rex is similarly fondly remembered, and indeed was personally commemorated in the Imperial War Museum's impressive 2006 exhibition The Animals' War. His Dickin Medal, badge and certificate – awarded during the same Wembley Stadium ceremony at which Thorn received his medal – were on display together with his harness and lead and a certificate of thanks for his later fundraising efforts for the charity.

Another Alsatian – the name itself a wartime invention to assuage anti-German feeling towards the breed – Rex was still a very young dog when he completed his training. Even so, according to an official report, when paired with his experienced handler Miss Dorothy Homan, 'Rex fully understands what is expected of him and he shows determination in exploration which has so often produced results.'

Before his training was complete Rex had already shown great natural ability, for example in January 1945 in south London, where he detected traces of blood well below the surface in an area of considerable destruction in Lambeth Road. Rescuers were inclined to ignore the dog's instincts, believing the blood to have fallen from victims being carried from the site. However, when Rex began pulling with his teeth at the debris, they renewed their efforts and eventually found a number of bodies, the presence of which had not been even suspected prior to the dog's arrival.

Two months later Rex and his handler were taken to the site of a burning factory to the west of London at Heston, and his performance was even more remarkable. When the decision was made to withdraw because part of the burning roof was collapsing, Rex resisted and according to the official report had physically to be dragged away until the fire was under control. Returned to the site shortly afterwards, when those parts not still burning were nevertheless very hot, the dog 'made his way his way across the debris in many places and gave indications of five casualties within four minutes'. Rex continued working to the best of his ability on two successive visits to the site. Even when he appeared to be sickening and was assumed to have 'suffered considerably from a heavy escape of gas', Rex carried on 'methodically searching the debris until the trainer withdrew him – obviously much against the dog's will'.

So often it was precisely this combination of skill, determination to perform to the best of their ability and sheer tenacity that achieved such good results. In this the best of the search-and-rescue dogs had much in common not just with their handlers but with everyone on the search teams. Combing the ruins of London, Coventry and so many other cities was painstaking and unpleasant war work but crucially important, and the task of finding casualties after each raid or rocket attack was made so much easier – and more effective – once these animals were brought onto the force.

Rex (L) and Thorn (R)

Peter
Scotch collie
Ministry of Aircraft Production (serving with Civil Defence)
Date of Award: 29 November 1945
For locating victims trapped under blitzed buildings while serving with the MAP attached to Civil Defence of London.

The last of the British dog world's 'magnificent seven', the pioneering heroes credited with saving hundreds of lives in the London Blitz. Peter was a Scotch collie of uncertain parentage but considerable talent, although it took a him a while to discover his true métier.

As a family pet Peter was a dead loss, acquired in 1941 for 25 shillings and by all accounts good for nothing besides disobeying instructions, scrapping with other dogs and wrecking the Birmingham home of his owner, Mrs Audrey Stables. Convinced she had been sold a pup in more senses than one, and describing her pet as a 'four-legged gangster', Mrs Stables was delighted to pass him on to the MAP in June 1944 when the call went out for volunteer dogs to report to RAF Woodfold. Finding himself under the care of trainer and handler Archie Knight, Peter quickly revealed a hitherto unsuspected capacity for learning and following instructions. Steadfast and able to keep his head under simulated battle conditions, and showing a real mastery of crucial new life-saving techniques, he was shortly afterwards posted with Mr Knight to Cranmer Court in London.

Officially Rescue Dog No. 2664/9288, Peter now found himself one of a team of 15 dogs searching for V-1 and V-2 casualties in the London Region Civil Defence area. He was quickly credited with six 'definites' as well as scores of 'probables', the latter term the usual euphemism employed at the time to describe victims killed by enemy action of this sort.

It was his speed and sagacity that marked Peter out, his accuracy enabling rescue squads to avoid many hours of fruitless digging. Admittedly on one occasion he was reported to have indicated an unusually articulate pet parrot when he and the rest of the team were clearly expecting to rescue a human being, rather more typical was his behaviour on 23 March 1945, when he worked hard and consistently well for nearly ten hours without a break. This was a remarkable period of sustained concentration for any dog let alone one with Peter's past reputation. All his 'marks' revealed casualties and after a very few hours' rest he was returned to the site and continued giving positive indications, enabling rescue workers to pull yet more victims from the wreckage.

The official account of the incident concludes by saying 'There is no doubt that the prompt and accurate information given by Peter to his handler resulted in at least three persons being rescued alive by the Rescue Squads.' This tells only part of the story, however, Archie Knight recollecting that the two of them were only called in '20 hours after the incident, and after several hours of heavy rain. Three bodies were missing, and [Peter] very quickly indicated in a most unlikely spot; but he was right, and they uncovered a man and a woman both on the same spot. After all that rain had packed the debris tightly, I thought this a most praiseworthy effort . . . He was really played out, but he worked like a Trojan.'

Occasionally Peter's gangster spirit showed itself, but even here one is left with a positive impression of his character rather than any sense of a dog returning to his bad old ways. Towards the very end of the war, for example, Peter and another of the 15, a dog called Taylor, began to show a dramatically reduced interest in the job. Neither Wright nor Taylor's handler could work out what the problem was until the latter suggested that the two had gone on strike. Heavy enemy action over the past week had delayed deliveries of supplies to the barracks at Cranmer Court, and faced with a diet of biscuits and water Peter and Taylor had responded in the only way they knew how. Once their meat ration was restored, the two returned to work, Peter shortly afterwards rescuing a small child after one of the very last rocket attacks of the war.

In late November 1945, following a glowing report to the Mascot Club, Peter was presented with his Dickin Medal during a ceremony at the Grosvenor House Hotel in Park Lane. Sir James Ross, secretary of the Air Ministry, made the presentation, and the following June the dog who for years refused even to walk to heel was chosen to lead the Civil Defence Stand Down Parade. This took place in Hyde Park on 10 June, and like Thorn and Rex before him Peter was presented to the King and Queen. According to a report in the *Birmingham Post & Mail* Peter received a kiss on the nose from the Queen – in whose fox fur he had shown a great interest – and a pat from the young Princess Elizabeth. He was then returned to Staverton Court, the new home of the MAP Guard Dog School. In July he was finally demobbed and returned to Mrs Stables, remaining with her until his death in November 1952 at the Nottingham branch of PDSA.

Peter was later buried at the Ilford PDSA Animal Cemetery, his exploits hitting the press again in July 2000 when his Dickin Medal was sent for auction at a large Spink sale of orders, decorations, medals and other militaria. Offered with a huge collection of supporting material, including the report cited above, the lot also included what the catalogue described as a '*superb* album of related documentation and photographs . . . representing a very vivid picture of Peter's wartime career and the background to his award'. Together with a signed certificate from the Royal Air Force, acknowledging Peter's 'Loyal and Faithful Service' and signed by the Force's provost marshal, this fitting and moving memoral to Peter and to Archie Knight realised £4,600.

Chapter 11

Lost and Found: Hell on High Ground

There are many hundreds of World War II crash sites around the United Kingdom, ranging from that of a Hawker Hurricane of 504 Squaron RAF, which was buried for decades beneath a crossroads in central London, to a crashed Consolidated Catalina flying boat lying in a remote spot on the Shetland island of Yell. Aside from the attendant tragedy (and the disgraceful pillaging of such sites by souvenir hunters) they bear mute but powerful witness to the shockingly high rate of casualties among British and Allied aircrews. These were men who so nearly made it home but who died on what could and should have been almost their final approach.

The Hurricane crashed after its heroic pilot, Sergeant Ray Holmes, with no ammunition remaining, rammed a German bomber heading for Buckingham Palace. He was fortunate and survived. Many of those who did not were returning to base in badly damaged aircraft after bombing, reconnaissance and other missions against Germany. Others found themselves too low on fuel to reach a viable runway, or unable to control their aircraft with wings and engines iced up. Some aircraft were flown by pilots lost or confused in bad weather, flying over unfamiliar territory or injured, or in conditions of appalling visibility.

Efforts to map and catalogue these many sites have been ongoing since the 1960s, although even now there is no real understanding of the numbers involved let alone the circumstances in which the individual aircraft were lost. Part of the problem is its sheer scale – my own county of Suffolk is known to have more than 1,000 such sites – while other estimates indicate that throughout the war years the effects of mechanical failure or human error brought about by fatigue, overconfidence and (not infrequently) inexperience may have led to the loss of as many as ten aircraft every day. Whatever the cause, the death toll which resulted provides yet another silent but terrible testimony to the unrelenting tragedy of total war.

With the war ongoing, and for much of the time aircraft falling to earth like shot pigeons, the hard-pressed authorities were rarely able to do little beyond recovering bodies where this was possible and any live ordnance which may have survived the impact. Enemy aircraft brought down or crash-landed were more closely scrutinised however for any intelligence value they might yield. This was especially the case where Messerschmidts, Focke-Wulfs and Junkers 88s were found in sufficiently good shape to be repaired and flown again and for a while over Lincolnshire, after being repainted with RAF roundels, several captured Luftwaffe aircraft were to be seen fighting it out with Hurricanes and 'Spits'. Equipped with cameras in place of guns and flown by British pilots, the aim was to improve Allied dogfighting tactics by improving our understanding of the enemy's capabilities.

In fact quite staggering losses continued until well after the war, so that as late as the period from May 1956 to January 1957 for example – barely eight months – 34 military aircraft were lost over the UK together with 42 aircrew, equivalent to one fatality roughly every six days.

Extraordinarily, it has in the main been left to aviation hobbyists and amateur archaeologists – often working many decades later – to discover what it was that went wrong on the day, who the crew members were, and in the event that any of them managed to parachute to safety and survive, what happened to them subsequently.

One rare exception to this is the case of a group of young American flyers who went down in the ferocious cold of a Cheviot winter, and the fact that their terrible story became so well known is largely due to a couple of very brave men and a brilliantly determined PDSA Dickin Medal-winning dog.

Sheila
Collie
Date of Award: 2 July 1945
For assisting in the rescue of four American Airmen lost on the Cheviots in a blizzard after an air crash in December, 1944.

Close to the spot where the Pennine Way eventually peters out, more than 280 miles from its start point down at Edale in the Peak District, the magnificent and remote Cheviot Hills straddle the frontier between the old kingdom of Northumbria and the Scottish border. Today they are a veritable graveyard for World War II aircraft.

In 1995, to mark the 50th anniversary of D-Day, a memorial to the men who lost their lives here was unveiled at the Sutherland Hall entrance to College Valley by His Royal Highness the Duke of Gloucester. The memorial is a sombre black monolith within a stone-walled stell or sheep pen. On the top of the monolith is an orientation map showing the location of the known crash sites for walkers who wish to visit these typically lonely, windswept locations. The memorial also includes details of the aircraft, a list which over the course of six years came to include a Spitfire and a Hurricane as well as a pair of Vickers Wellingtons, Lancaster, Hampden, Stirling and Halifax bombers, and an example of Britain's famous 'wooden wonder' the elegant and highly effective de Havilland Mosquito.

Although the area is often treacherous underfoot, and the weather frequently extreme, by no means were lives lost on every occasion, and the memorial was erected not just to the airmen but also to give thanks to the shepherds, farmers and other local men and women who on each occasion turned out and helped with the rescue efforts.

Among the luckier airmen to be rescued in this way were several but sadly not all the crew members of USAF Boeing B-17G Flying Fortress 44-6504, which had taken off from the Eighth Air Force base at RAF Molesworth in Cambridgeshire. The aircraft subsequently became lost after running into a blizzard on 16 December 1944 while returning with a full payload from an aborted bombing raid on an important railway marshalling yard at Ulm in Germany.

After the mission was called off due to the deteriorating weather, a total of 39 heavy bombers from 303rd Bomb Group (H) – nicknamed Hell's Angels – were ordered to break formation over the Low Countries. In order to cut the risk of mid-air collision the nine-man crews were told to head for separate bases across the UK. The pilot of 44-6504, Lieutenant George A. Kyle, requested bearings back to England but, apparently misled by rogue signals from German transmitters, at one point found himself flying south towards France. He eventually ended up too far north to reach any suitable airbase in England.

Realising this as he made landfall over Seahouses on the Northumberland coast, Kyle made an attempt to descend through the low cloud to establish visible bearings. He did this in the hope that he could put the aircraft down in a forced landing, but unfortunately the manoeuvre meant the B-17 was now too low to clear the snow-covered Cheviots, which at their peak on the Cheviot itself rise to some 2,674 feet.

At approximately 13.15 the Flying Fortress crashed-landed on West Hill beneath the summit before sliding across a peat bog and coming to a halt on the hill shoulder. Remarkably the bombs on the aircraft remained intact for the time being but the impact as the plane came down into Braydon Crag was nevertheless heard by several local people living further down the hill. These included a working shepherd from Dunsdale, John Dagg, who had served in the Great War as a decorated private in the King's Own Scottish Borderers. His 11-year-old son, also called John, was with him at the time.

Having assisted with a rescue in the area following a crash the previous year, the father lost no time in setting out for the hill with his collie Sheila, leaving his wife and young son to contact the authorities and tell them what had happened.

There is no easy way to reach Braydon Crag, a large rocky outcrop which as the crow flies is more than three miles from the nearest public road at Cocklawfoot, and on an already blustery afternoon conditions were rapidly worsening. Dagg could not see the crash site but he could hear and smell the fires that had erupted around the bomber's ruptured hydraulic and fuel lines. Together with Frank Moscrop, another shepherd from Southernknowe whom he encountered on the way up, Dagg made his way towards the general area. Sheila had by this time disappeared after going on ahead.

By the time the two men neared the site, after what the official record in the *London Gazette* subsequently described as 'a strenuous climb in heavy snow', the dog had succeeded in locating four of the crew, who were sheltering from the bitter cold in a crevice in the peat. Returning to her master, Sheila led him back to Sergeants Howard Delaney, George Smith, William R. Kaufmann and Joel Berly. Although unable to explain what had happened to their missing colleagues, the dazed and freezing crew were at least able to warn the two local men not to approach the wreckage. By now this was burning fiercely, and of course it still contained a full complement of bombs.

Two of the four were badly injured, so Dagg administered some basic first aid. As all four were barefoot he also helped wrap their feet in material recovered from a parachute, and after searching briefly for the remaining crew men began to lead the small party down the hill to relative safety. By this time, as the *London Gazette* was later to note, 'a blizzard was blowing which rendered visibility practically nil'. Because of this the descent proved horrendously difficult, and it was only through what the official report termed 'dogged perseverance, patience and tenacity of purpose that the rescuers were able to get the four men to safety'.

Happily it transpired that three of the remaining crewmen, including the badly injured pilot, had managed to find their own way down to Mounthooly in College Valley, and on reaching Dagg's cottage they and the shepherds heard an explosion from the wreckage. This was sufficiently loud to shatter a couple of windows down below, so clearly had the crew still been in the immediate vicinity of the aircraft they might well have died. At this point – and despite their evident exhaustion after some seven hours struggling against the elements – Dagg, Moscrop and Sheila immediately set off back up the hillside to look for the two last crewmen, who were still unaccounted for.

They were soon beaten back by the weather, however, and with night falling the trio was forced to postpone all further efforts until the morning. At daybreak Dagg made another ascent, at the conclusion of which he and Sheila discovered the bodies of the two missing crewmen, Sergeant Frank Roderick Turner Junior and Flight Officer Fred Holcombe. Killed when the nose section of the aircraft had smashed into the ground, the navigator and bombardier's bodies were lying close to the burned-out carcass of the B-17.

In the words of the *Gazette*, with both men and the dog having shown 'great courage in facing a blizzard on the Cheviot with constant danger from deep snow-drifts, there is little doubt that their bravery, skill and determination were instrumental in saving the lives of four airmen from death by exposure'. On the recommendation of the Home Office, Sheila's name was put forward for her to receive the 24th Dickin Medal, the first such honour to be conferred on a civilian animal. Dagg and Moscrop were each awarded the British Empire Medal 'for Meritorious Service' as well as scrolls from the grateful US Eighth Air Force to officially recognise and thank them for their heroic endeavours.

The medals and scrolls were presented to the two men at a hillside ceremony the following July by Sir James Ross, representing the Air Ministry, and Colonel E. A. Romig of the United States Air Force. The same day Sheila, having been enrolled as Honorary Member No. 1103 of the Allied Forces Mascot Club, was presented with her Dickin Medal by Lady Ross. The award included an extra length of ribbon for her collar, on the sensible assumption that a working dog would not wear the medal except on rare occasions.

The story of the rescue and the unique awards to both man and beast of medals for gallantry was to reverberate down the years. For a long time the Dagg family remained in close contact with the parents of the dead airmen and offered to tend the two graves at nearby Kirknewton Cemetery. (Both bodies were subsequently moved to the large American cemetery near Cambridge.) Also, in August 1946, in response to a letter from Sergeant Turner's mother Sallie, the younger John offered to send the Turners one of Sheila's puppies, a near-white bitch named Tibby, although when news of the transatlantic offer leaked to the press she was more often referred to as Sheila II.

The offer was quickly accepted, and after being boxed up and labelled 'Be good to Tibby' the little dog set off for South Carolina courtesy of TWA. With considerable fanfare from newspapers on both sides of the Atlantic, she was met at New York's LaGuardia Field by the couple's niece, Jean Turner, and when last heard of was reported as having won 'best cared-for dog' at a local dog show.

In December 1994, on the 50th anniversary of the disaster, two F-15s from the USAF 48th Fighter Wing at RAF Lakenheath in Suffolk performed a fly-past in memory of the lost airmen, passing low over West Hill at precisely 13.15. Then, on a rare sunny day in October 2005, following the death of the B-17's pilot at his home in Fort Lauderdale, the story resurfaced again when George Kyle's daughter, an old friend and the son of his co-pilot returned to the Cheviot. They were there to fulfil Kyle's last wish to have his ashes scattered at the site where he had lost two comrades and where he had himself had the narrowest of escapes.

The same year coin and medal specialists Morton & Eden announced in association with Sotheby's a sale of medals, orders and decorations to be held in Bond Street on 13 December. Among the lots was Sheila's Dickin Medal, together with her master's Great War medals, his BEM and an incredible wealth of supporting material. The lot also included several of the many letters that passed between the Dagg, Holcombe and Turner families, correspondence from Buckingham Palace to John Dagg, a letter signed by Maria Elizabeth Dickin relating to the rescue and, in a somewhat melancholy coda, an offer from the PDSA to Mr Dagg of a plot for Sheila in Ilford when the time came. (This was never taken up, however, and Sheila was eventually buried at home in Northumberland.)

The estimate was high – £20–30,000 – doubtless in part because of the comprehensive nature of Lot 215 as well as its international dimension and the irresistibly moving story that surrounds it. In the end the collection – together making what the auctioneer called 'a lovely tale with a great deal of interest' – was knocked down for an incredible £23,500. While the buyer chose to remain anonymous, it is known that this extraordinary collection has remained in the area where the shattered silver-grey remains of the B-17 still lie.

Chapter 12

A Tale of Three Horses

Between 1914 and 1918 a quite shocking eight million war horses were killed by disease, exposure, starvation, shell- or gunfire, although the gradual introduction of British and French tanks during that same period looked likely to reduce the military's reliance on such animals in future conflicts. This was achieved eventually, but only in the face of considerable resistance from hippophilic conservatives, who despite the evidence of their own eyes retained an almost mystical devotion to their mounts.

Notwithstanding these nostalgic yearnings, the 1920s saw the successful mechanisation of all British mounted cavalry regiments, although for many years afterwards cavalrymen continued to fight a rearguard action against the despised machines. Indeed as late as 1935 the minister for war, Duff Cooper, a former Grenadier guards officer, was still blimpishly insisting that the well-bred horse would always find a role in warfare. Neither were the other services better: at the same time many of those who had learned to fly in biplanes affected to find something slightly sinister and un-English about the latest designs for faster, more efficient and more agile monoplanes.

The last charge by a full British cavalry unit in fact took back in 1920, when the 20th Hussars successfully routed a body of Turkish infantry. This was during the Chanak Crisis, a now largely forgotten assault on French and British troops who had secured the Dardanelles. Some two decades later Sikh *sowars* of the Burma Frontier Force charged a detachment of Japanese at Toungoo, but this final hurrah for the imperial horse in March 1942 involved only a relatively modest patrol of horsemen, probably no more than 60 strong. The same year also saw what will likely prove to be the very last mounted charge by any military force, on 23 August at Izbushensky on the River Don. This involved some 600 lancers of the Italian Savoia cavalry regiment who charged approximately 2,000 Soviet infantry. Such a quixotic gesture was already far from the norm, however, and the Italians were anyway quickly driven back and with substantial casualites.

Unfortunately none of this meant that the horse was finished as a service animal. Quite phenomenal numbers continued to be employed on many fronts and by all sides throughout World War II – at least six million of them by the Germans and Russians alone – although increasingly the animals were involved in the transport of artillery, materiel and other supplies rather than anything a traditionalist would recognise as a cavalry role.

Similarly on the British home front horses continued to play an important part in keeping things moving, particularly in the capital, where the authorities have relied on mounted officers for a surprisingly long time.

London's first mounted force – the Bow Street Horse Patrol, of just eight animals and their riders – was created as long ago as the 1760s by Sir John Fielding, the celebrated eighteenth-century magistrate. Dressed in scarlet and blue with black leather stocks and hats, making them the first uniformed policemen anywhere in the world, Sir John's small squad was chiefly required to give protection from highwaymen on all main roads within 20 miles of Charing Cross. This role diminished with the coming of the railways, but the force gradually evolved to take on a number of new responsibilities, including keeping livestock thefts in check around the edges of the capital and taking messages from one side of it to the other.

By 1886, the year London policemen were issued with whistles instead of rattles, the capital's horsemen were being retrained again, this time in more substantial numbers and mostly now for riot control which was to remain a key task throughout London until well into the 1930s. The outbreak of another European war at the end of that decade seemed likely to reduce the threat from widespread civil disturbances, but from 1940 the destruction and devastation wrought by the German Luftwaffe was clearly going to create many new challenges for the police generally – and much of that load was to fall on the Mounted Branch.

Most obviously, with official forecasts of up to 30,000 casualties a day at the height of the bombing, greater strain would be placed on civilian administration and law enforcement. Admittedly the wardens of the newly created ARP service were expected to shoulder some of the burden, with a projected 200,000 volunteers and 16,000 full-time personnel, but police reservists and pensioners were also recalled to duty, and a new Women's Auxiliary Police Corps set up. Unexpectedly the Mounted Branch was at first kept clear of the chaos, its handsome if typically somewhat nervous creatures being shipped out to the country, many of them back to the branch's headquarters at Imber Court in Surrey and others to the stables at Kempton Park racecourse.

It took only a matter of weeks for the authorities to realise their error. The men were unhappy at being sidelined, and it was an obvious waste of resources. Within two months men and horses were duly returned to the capital. There they remained on duty, sharing the daily diet of anti-aircraft fire, incendiaries and flying bombs which was to become the lot of their fellow Londoners. These attacks which were to result in more than 80,000 deaths and serious injuries, well over half of the UK's civilian casualties over the course of the war.

In the course of these attacks a third of the historic City of London was laid waste, as was around a fifth of some inner-city boroughs such as Southwark and Stepney. Today it is hard to imagine the impact of all this on horses. Their training typically included deliberate and prolonged exposure to crowds and traffic noise, military bands and even small-arms fire, but they nevertheless still belong to a species which can be notoriously sensitive and nervous.

That said, they must somehow have become at least partly used to the sights, sounds and smells of war, particularly those stabled near the Metropolitan Police piggery in Hyde Park. (Many city-dwellers kept pigs for food during the war, including somewhat curiously the members of the Ladies' Carlton Club in Pall Mall, who converted their basement swimming pool into a temporary sty. The Met's was one of the larger ones, however, having been built by the officers themselves using timber from ruined buildings – which is to say looted material.)

The smell and noise of the piggery may have lent the park a certain rural touch, although from the horses' perspective this would have been more than countered by the sound of gunfire. Unfortunately this part of the royal park was also home to a battery of more than 130 immense 3.7-inch anti-aircraft guns, requiring the horses to become habituated to the deafening roar of often very drawn-out salvoes.

Initially some attempt was made to accustom them to the sound of air-raid sirens, so that for a brief while each horse was given an extra ration of feed whenever one of these went off. Unfortunately the sirens were soon sounding most days and around the clock – all told there were 1,124 alerts in the space of five years – and the practice had to be abandoned for reasons of both health and economy. Though it had been quick to establish, the horses' Pavlovian response to the sirens took a while to fade – but it is hard to believe that a few oats would really have done much to alleviate the effects of falling bombs, collapsing buildings or the ever-present threat of fire.

For all that, only one police horse is thought to have been killed in an air raid, and ironically the mount in question, called Regent, was at the time of the V-1 attack not in London but away on a training course in Surrey. Even so, for those horses and men on duty, the threat of death was very real. In the very worst areas of devastation the responsibility for keeping things moving lay entirely with the Mounted Branch while sites were being cleared and unexploded ordnance made safe.

In all some 186 horses saw service in London during the war years, a figure that compares well with today's Mounted Branch which typically keeps 120 animals for ceremonial, high-visibility and public order patrols. Much like search-and-rescue dogs, each of the wartime police horses was assigned to an individual officer, a man who would form a strong bond with his mount and then be expected to ride and work with that horse for the entirety of the animal's service life.

For much of the time the horses were well distributed around the capital, and the large Metropolitan Police Stables on the raised first floor at 7 Great Scotland Yard remained largely empty for the duration. This followed the realisation by a senior officer standing beneath the glass roof of its central courtyard that a single well-aimed bomb could potentially wipe out more than half the force. In the main they were engaged in unspectacular work: keeping the traffic moving, and by their presence providing reassurance to shell-shocked citizens. Their impressive ability to remain calm in situations where most horses would have bolted also helped calm the many others still employed pulling cabs and wagons around London's streets, and of course made it possible for their riders to perform their own duties at a time when London and Londoners badly needed order and some sense of normality.

As the author and administrator C. P. Snow memorably put it, the war years were when most people's preoccupations were 'equally divided between what they were going to eat today and what was going to happen in Britain tomorrow'. Whatever else was happening in the world, and in the skies above our cities, life had to carry on – and not infrequently it fell to the men and horses of the Met to see that it did. Eventually three horses were recommended for a PDSA Dickin Medal, all of them thoroughly deserving cases but apparently chosen very much as representatives of the entire force rather than for any single outstanding action or event.

Olga
Police horse
Date of Award: 11 April 1947
On duty when a flying bomb demolished four houses in Tooting and a plate-glass window crashed immediately in front of her. Olga, after bolting for 100 yards, returned to the scene of the incident and remained on duty with her rider, controlling traffic and assisting rescue organisations.

*

Olga and Ricky the dog (page 58)

The example of Olga serves – besides much else – to remind us that we should perhaps expect no more of an animal than that it should flee when faced with extreme danger.

Patrolling in south London on 3 July 1944, Olga was without her usual rider when a V-1 flying bomb fell on Besley Street SW16, close to the railway line from Streatham to Tooting. The nature of such weapons meant that women and children were especially likely to find themselves victims, something which made them seem even more sinister. The fact that they were unmanned also made them somehow worse, the novelist Evelyn Waugh being far from alone in finding them 'as impersonal as the plague, as though the city was infested with enormous, venomous insects'.

For months at a time seemingly every dawn brought a new and terrible toll: more craters in the streets, gaping holes where once homes had stood, and more bodies to pull from the rubble and out of fires. Other cities faced similar challenges but nothing on the scale of London, and on this occasion the blast killed four people almost instantly while completely destroying a number of houses and seriously damaging several other buildings in the area. Less than 100 yards from the point of impact, Olga and her replacement rider PC J. E. Thwaites felt the blast directly, the horse bolting immediately afterwards when a large plate-glass window crashed to the ground immediately in front of her.

PC Thwaites was fortunately able quickly to bring her under control, and after reassuring her the pair were able to return to the scene of the devastation. As the first officer to arrive on site, Thwaites' job was to keep the area free of sightseers – it was the second such attack in the area in two days, but the public seemed never to tire of viewing the aftermath – while directing pedestrians and non-related traffic away from the blast area. Olga's exemplary behaviour meant Thwaites was able to perform his duties effectively so that the rescue services could reach the dead and injured as quickly as possible.

Upstart
Police horse
Date of Award: 11 April 1947
While on patrol duty in Bethnal Green a flying bomb exploded within 75 yards, showering both horse and rider with broken glass and debris. Upstart was completely unperturbed and remained quietly on duty with his rider controlling traffic, etc., until the incident had been dealt with.

Only a few weeks after the incident involving Olga, another horse, Upstart, was patrolling in Bethnal Green. He had been one of the horses stabled close to the ack-ack battery in Hyde Park until his box was badly damaged by enemy action. After this Upstart was transferred to new quarters to the east of the City, but unfortunately to an area which was to sustain considerably more damage than his former billet.

For the Luftwaffe east London was an obvious target, with a higher concentration of industry than most other parts of the capital, much denser housing (meaning the effect of their bombs in terms of death and destruction was potentially much greater than in the leafy suburbs), and of course it was home to most of the docks. In fact east London literally felt the heat when the docks south of the river were hit too: on 7 September 1940, when 1.5 million tons of wood stored at the Surrey Commercial Docks went up, paint blistered on boats moored hundreds of yards away on the opposite side of the river.

By the time of Upstart's arrival in Bethnal Green, the impressively stoical locals already had some experience of the V-1, as just after 04.00 on 13 June 1944 six residents of the borough had become the very first flying-bomb fatalities of the war. (This unwanted distinction is now commemorated by an official English Heritage blue plaque affixed to the railway bridge over Grove Road, E3.) Early V-1s were not particularly effective, however: of the first ten launched half crashed almost immediately and a sixth was lost in the Channel. On another occasion one actually bounced off Tower Bridge – some reports claimed it had actually passed above the road but below the walkways – before sinking a nearby tug. Fortunately the iconic structure itself more or less undamaged.

Although their fear was genuine, the public was also quick to grasp the reality of the situation. This was that the pilotless planes were more expensive than conventional bombers and less effective, and as such almost certainly represented a last-gasp effort from Germany. Nor was the Royal Air Force slow in coming up with a solution, at least once its new Hawker Tempest proved fast enough to enable skilled pilots such as Wing Commander Roland Beaumont to fly alongside the 450 mph doodlebugs before tipping them off course with a flick of a wing. In all Beaumont is known to have derailed more than 30 V-1s in this way, and was subsequently being hailed by the London *Evening Standard* as the key defender of the capital against this particular technology.

For the time being they were still deadly, however, and on 22 August 1944 another one found its mark in the streets of east London. As one of nine to hit the area between Bethnal Green and Shoreditch in a very short space of time it was a devastating blow. Patrolling with her rider DI J. Morley, Upstart was close enough to the seat of the explosion for both to be showered with glass and debris, although fortunately neither was seriously hurt. The devastation was nevertheless considerable, and it fell to Morley as the man at the scene to clear the way for ARP and ambulance personnel to reach the casualties and to secure the area until it was made safe. For Morley to control the situation he needed Upstart to remain calm and on station, something the horse was able to do, having perhaps learned from his experiences of living so close to an AA battery that a loud noise while unpleasant is itself survivable.

Such scenes were often truly horrific, but occasionally Morley and his colleagues had to deal with situations which now sound almost comedic. Faced with the most obvious hazards, civilians could be spectacularly foolish, and when one man was fined £100 by Westminster magistrates after being caught dragging a small unexploded bomb down Jermyn Street – he said he intended dumping it in Green Park – it was an unusual case but by no means unique.

Mostly though police work of this sort meant keeping traffic flowing around the scene of a disaster and moving on unwanted spectators. As early as December 1940 there were an estimated

3,000 unexploded bombs (UXBs) in the capital, each one needing to be deactivated once the police had helped evacuate everyone living within 600 yards. The mounted police were also charged with preventing looters and souvenir hunters from entering ruins – something so-called bomb-chasers continued to do even though the crime was in theory punishable by death. Depressingly even rescue workers succumbed from time to time, and nearly half of all arrests made by police at new bombsites involved Civil Defence members caught pinching things for themselves.

Possibly the opportunities were simply too tempting for many to resist, and of course the likelihood of being caught was that much lower when the police had more pressing duties to deal with. Crime definitely rose during the war years and, although it was observed that when a V-1 blew the doors off a cinema in Clapham no one attempted to get in without paying, looting in 1944 was certainly much worse than in 1941 and 1942. Even so, it was more of a substantial crime ripple than an actual wave, with around 15 per thousand Londoners reportedly involved in criminality in 1944 compared to just 10 per thousand six years previously.

Regal
Police horse
Date of Award: 11 April 1947
Was twice in burning stables caused by explosive incendiaries at Muswell Hill. Although receiving minor injuries, being covered by debris and close to the flames, this horse showed no signs of panic.

The third and so far at least final equine recipient of the Dickin Medal, Regal was based not in the inner city but in suburban north London at police stables in Muswell Hill.

On 19 April 1941, together with the nearby church of St James, the stables were badly damaged by fire when German incendiary bombs rained down on many parts of the suburb. One clutch fell close to the police station, starting a fire in the forage room, which thanks to an abundance of highly inflammable hay and hessian sacking quickly spread to the stables themselves. Regal remained calm as the flames crept closer and closer, and allowed himself to be led to safety when help at last arrived. The same extraordinary self-control was evident three years later. On 20 July 1944 – coincidentally the day Hitler narrowly escaped the best attempt yet to blow him up – the building was again badly damaged, this time by a V-1 falling just yards down the street. This time the horse was injured, hit by glass and debris as the roof of the station partially collapsed, but as was observed at the time – Regal by name and regal by nature – 'he once again lived up to his name . . . and was not unduly perturbed'.

As noted previously there is nothing like a calm horse to prevent other horses from panicking, and London at this time was still home to around 40,000 of the animals with many living in the East End and around the docks. Across the capital an estimated 4,000 horses and ponies were also still employed pulling milk floats, and incredibly the last horse-drawn taxi, a four-wheeled 'growler' operating from Victoria Station, was retired only in 1947. When these working horses were injured or trapped or just plain terrified by the noise of war it frequently fell to the men and horses of the Mounted Branch to rescue the situation, something they did time and again.

It should also be noted that by 1944 the police were receiving rather less help than they had done earlier from the Civil Defence authorities, thereby making the job of the Mounted Branch harder still. In 1943 with the Blitz apparently now behind them – and plenty of rumours but no proof yet of the existence of the V-1 and V-2 – the authorities in London cut the budget for Civil Defence services from just over £14 million to £8.3 million. Also many who had joined the ARP were now growing old or were disabled, while more than 15 per cent of personnel – being female – found themselves largely confined to office duties rather than helping out on the streets.

What Civil Defence could no longer cover the police had to, and once air attacks restarted in earnest their job got worse and worse. Even so, with 101 daylight raids on London, 253 night attacks and an astonishing 30,000 houses in the capital destroyed by V-1 and V-2 blasts (and another 1.25 million badly damaged) it took far longer than it should have for the police's important contribution to be recognised officially.

Not until 1947 – after several mounted officers had attended the PDSA Chelsea Show – was the decision made to award Dickin Medals to the three horses named here. Even then a fourth animal was inexplicably passed over – Ubique, whose sixth sense was widely said to have prevented his rider walking into the path of an oncoming flying bomb – but eventually the ceremony took place. It was held in Hyde Park in the presence of Major General Sir John Marriott, district officer commanding London District, and Metropolitan Police Commissioner Sir Harold Scott.

Thereafter all three remained in the service until their retirement, and as Dickin Medal recipients they would automatically have been granted a plot at Ilford when the time came. This entitlement was not taken up, however, and when the time came the three were instead interred at Thames Ditton, close to Imber Court. A small museum on the site commemorates the long history of the Mounted Branch, and includes among the exhibits all three Dickin Medals and a small collection of related memorabilia.

Chapter 13

Ground Zero

Building on lessons learned during the Blitz and from many natural disasters in the years since, civilian authorities at home and abroad have continued to depend on specialist dogs when it comes to search, rescue and recovery situations.

The most recent search-and-rescue dog to be honoured with the award of a PDSA Dickin Medal is Appollo, a German shepherd recruited and trained in urban search and rescue by the New York Police Department's K-9 Unit. In 2001 he was reportedly hard at work in the ruins of the twin towers within 15 minutes of the September 11 attacks, one of more than 300 dogs eventually brought in to work at Ground Zero. With no hope of survivors, the animals and their courageous handlers and owners were instead charged with the painstaking and uniquely grim task of scouring the devastated site of the World Trade Center for often minute physical traces of the three thousand victims.

Over the following months other animals, including many specifically trained therapy dogs, were to provide help of another kind, giving crucial emotional support to both rescue workers and the families of the victims. Understandably much of the focus of news and other media remained fixed on those dogs that had arrived at the scene early on, however, and on those who were filmed and photographed carrying out their work in the first few days of the disaster.

According to the Federal Emergency Management Agency (FEMA) the breeds present at Ground Zero included German, Belgian and Australian shepherds, Labradors and retrievers, Portuguese waterdogs, German pointers, Belgian Malinois and Tervurens, Border collies, poodles, Dobermann pinschers, giant schnauzers, rat terriers and a variety of what in the US they call pound puppies. But this list notwithstanding, the 300 or so formed a largely homogenous group in terms of breeds – Labradors and retrievers seem very much to have predominated – although they and their handlers had rushed to Manhattan from all over the continental United States.

Moxie, for example, a three-year-old chocolate Labrador, travelled from Winthrop, Massachussetts; another older Lab called Tara came from nearby Ipswich, and the two-year-old German shepherd Kaiser arrived within hours of the tragedy from Indianapolis, nearly 650 miles away. With their respective handlers, Mark Aliberti, Lee Prentiss and Tony Zintsmaster, the three dogs were eventually to spend a full eight days searching the dangerous smoking ruins. Others came from even further afield, and in some cases stayed much longer: Bretagne from Texas, Guinness from Highland, California, Hoke from Denver; offers even came from dog handlers in Vancouver, British Columbia. At the same time many other handlers were deployed with their dogs to the

Pentagon and to the Flight 93 crash site near Stony Creek in Pennsylvania.

Searches at each location went on day and night, with the dogs' 12-hour shifts soon extended to 16 and more once recovery rather than rescue had been recognised as the sole objective. One German shepherd, Hansen, and his NYPD handler Officer Steve Smaldon, were to spend around 150 days at Ground Zero before eventually being stood down.

Most of the dogs are sadly now gone. Every dog lover knows that the largest breeds rarely enjoy the longest lifespans, and many of America's hero dogs developed strange immune-system responses after spending time at Ground Zero. Fortunately these appeared mostly to be temporary, but who is to say what the long-term ramifications are of such a dangerous and toxic environment. It was after all a place where, as one survivor put it, there was initially more dust and debris to breathe than there was air.

There was also another kind of atmosphere to contend with, an atmosphere that led one handler to note how at the end of a shift his dog 'kind of withdrew from everything, there was so much death'. Even now, in so many photographs taken at the time, one can almost see this withdrawal in their eyes; but then again other dogs at Ground Zero, apparently brushing aside the effects of such problems, emotional and physical, went on to perform equally sterling service following the destruction of the Katrina and Rita hurricanes in 2005.

Speaking very soon after the 9/11 attacks, Bob Sessions, a rescue worker with FEMA, which had scores of its own trained and certified dogs on site, spoke for many when he said, 'If these dogs only knew what a difference they make ... Certainly there's nothing that can replace the precision of a dog's nose – and absolutely nothing that can replace a dog's heart.' Most dog owners would recognise such a sentiment immediately, and indeed in the early days at Ground Zero at least one hard-pressed fire-fighter was clearly genuinely touched when the aforementioned Bretagne, a three year-old golden retriever, comforted him as he paused amid the rubble to catch his breath. Another wept tears of gratitude when a dog located the remains of a colleague, and workers at all three locations were periodically to be observed sneaking a few minutes' rest in the company of one dog or another. Without doubt, while these dogs were not able to save any lives – there were none to be saved – their presence enabled them to provide real comfort and some genuine solace for the firefighters and other professionals working at the scene.

Something very similar was seen in London in the 1940s. Those who witnessed Blitz dogs – trained or untrained, official war dogs and adopted street urchins alike – never failed to be impressed by what they saw.

Even the most experienced urban search-and-rescue workers were repeatedly surprised at what the dogs were able to achieve when faced with the unprecedented devastation of 9/11. Once a scent was detected, noted one searcher at the scene, a good dog would scout endlessly until called to stand down. Another described how impressive it was to see how 'they go underneath into void spaces – anywhere we can get the dogs in. The site is very difficult . . . for the dogs [so] they're crawling in on their bellies and squeezing through things. It's incredible.'

Visiting the scene on 14 September, President George W. Bush was photographed greeting one search dog and the image was flashed around the world. Even so, the role of dogs in the 9/11 story is still little known in Britain, although in the US the dogs have received much more of the credit they so clearly deserve. In New York's Suffolk County, for example, at Lindenhurst, the dogs have their own commemorative statue – a large bronze of one of the German shepherds from the area who worked at Ground Zero.

More recently, to mark the tenth anniversary of the attacks, photographer Charlotte Dumas has published a series of homely but honest and deeply moving portraits of the surviving search dogs. After an odyssey which saw her criss-crossing the US from Texas to Maryland to track down the 15 still surviving, countless newspaper articles, magazine stories and popular dog blogs have commemorated the dogs' achievements by continuing to explore the relationships that developed between rescuers called to the site and those who assisted them. The best of these, and there are many, successfully capture the very real and enduring contribution made in the hours, days and weeks that followed the first impact at 08.46 that dreadful morning.

Strictly speaking what the whole world now knows as 9/11 was a peacetime atrocity rather than a military action of the type Maria Dickin envisaged six decades earlier. Like those medal recipients who went before them, however – and indeed the hundreds of other animals honoured at one remove by those awards – the dogs described here, Appollo, Roselle and Salty each displayed genuine courage and unswervable devotion, which for most is sufficient. A bright light on the darkest of days, if nothing else their examples underline again how not all heroes are human, and reading their stories now none surely would deny the three and the hundreds like them the claim, 'We Also Serve.'

Appollo
German shepherd
New York Police dog representing all the Search and Rescue dogs at Ground Zero and the Pentagon
Date of Award: 5 March 2002
For tireless courage and unstinting devotion to duty during the search-and-rescue operations at Ground Zero and the Pentagon

following the terrorist attacks on New York and Washington on 11 September 2001. Faithful to words of command and undaunted by the task, the dog's work and unstinting devotion to duty stand as a testament to those lost or injured.

Chosen by ballot to represent the several hundred search-and-rescue dogs who worked so well and so hard at Ground Zero and the other crash sites, Appollo and his popular handler New York Police Department Officer Peter Davis were the first K-9 unit to attend the disaster site in Lower Manhattan.

Davis and the German shepherd, at that time coming up to his tenth birthday, were on site within minutes of the second tower's collapse, a time of extreme if unknowable danger. With debris still falling, the air thick with toxic smoke choking, dust and worse, and understandable panic and chaos in and around the area of heaviest devastation, the two of them went straight to work.

According to Lieutenant Dan Donadio, canine team chief of the NYPD Emergency Service Unit, Davis and Appollo 'went right on the pile. Some rubble gave way under the dog . . . and flames shot up around him'. Appollo was undaunted. Like his handler and the other dogs which soon joined them, he kept going regardless of the threat to his own safety, eventually turning in the first of many unbroken 12-hour shifts spent sifting through the ruins of the two towers looking for human remains.

'They have to be the longest-working, most hard-working dogs ever,' recalled Donadio in interviews about the earliest days of the recovery operation. In overall charge of the canine team, and having himself arrived within the first hour of the disaster. Donadio was eventually to spend more than nine months at the scene. Describing the dogs as 'New York's most faithful', he counts himself lucky to have witnessed their quite extraordinary response to this unparalleled tragedy.

Certified by FEMA as a Level I canine – one of only 25 dogs in the United States at the time to operate at such a level – Appollo had joined his NYPD unit back in 1994. As a youngster his training was not just in search and rescue but also involved weapons recovery, criminal apprehension, routine patrol work and cadaver recovery. Tragically it was the latter skill that now came to the fore, and to those watching Appollo at work, handlers and other rescue workers alike, it was immediately apparent that the many months of training and play involved in producing a K-9 dog had more than paid off.

Like London's Blitz dogs before them, Appollo and scores of others were able to move quickly over the twisted steel and shattered glass, navigating the site with ease. Seemingly oblivious to the dangers, some even walked the makeshift narrow pathways of beams stretched over burning voids many metres below. That there was no fixed organisation in place initially seemed not to matter, and similarly the lack of reliable illumination when the first night fell scarcely held them back. Understanding instinctively what was expected of them, the dogs just put their heads down and got on with the task in hand.

Inevitably this initial ad hoc approach meant that it was hugely dangerous, and Appollo was almost certainly not alone in having at least one very close brush with death. When a firefighter asked Officer Davis to assist with a search in a particular area, Appollo slipped through loose debris down into one of several dangerous voids, one containing a body of deep water which had collected from the many disabled fire hydrants around the 16-acre site. Moments later flames shot up from the ruins and the dog reappeared dotted with burning embers, which Davis quickly brushed off. Having accidentally but fortunately been well doused with water just moments earlier, Appollo escaped serious injury and was almost immediately back at work quartering the location indicated by the firefighter.

With such dangers ever present while clambering around on what became known as 'the pile', considerable efforts were soon made to safeguard the dogs as they went about their work. Canine supply companies provided hundreds of sets of protective boots, showing great ingenuity when closed borders and grounded aircraft initially threatened to interrupt deliveries. Others were donated by ordinary Americans, who started making them at home when it became apparent how quickly the dogs were wearing them out. The New York Center for Animal Care and Control also received what it described as 'more dog food than we can possibly use'.

While work continued combing through more than a million tons of hazardous debris at Ground Zero, and later at a massive landfill site on Staten Island, mobile veterinary hospitals were being established to care for both working dogs and the many other animals found abandoned around the crash sites or belonging to the dead and missing. Hundreds of dogs, cats, rabbits, guinea pigs, ferrets and even reptiles were rescued in this way, and in another echo of wartime Britain (and the mobile PDSA Rescue Squads described in Chapter 10) strays and rescue animals alike were soon receiving expert professional treatment for shock, dehydration and respiratory distress.

During the long period of the recovery operation an estimated 250 volunteer vets are thought to have been involved in this way. Attempts were also made to head off potential problems by giving all the dogs on site preventative antibiotics and examining each of them at the end of every shift to check their coats and eyes for damage from the smoke and dust. Although only two dogs were required to stand down as a result of these examinations, such care was to prove vital in an environment where humans were provided with every kind of protective clothing but the dogs were expected to push their faces and noses deep into the contaminated debris.

It was also recognised that some of the animals would suffer emotionally too, and on the evidence of those who knew them best many appeared to have done so. Just as in wartime London, where Crumstone Irma had responded very differently to a corpse than to a victim who was merely injured (see page 181), the toll of finding nothing but the dead eventually began to show here too.

At one point, for example, Officer Davis was convinced that Appollo was becoming frustrated by the work, that the dog was actually growing disheartened at never finding anyone alive that he could rescue. Davis persuaded a fellow NYPD officer to hide in the rubble so that Appollo could find him and get the credit for the 'rescue'. The ruse was simple enough but worked like a charm, the dog redoubling his efforts following his successful find and after witnessing his handler's positive response to the 'discovery'. These dogs clearly want to help, after all, but sometimes it seems they too need help.

The decision to recognise the dogs' achievements with a Dickin Medal was perhaps a natural one, and Appollo was evidently a popular choice once the results of the ballot became known. The award was made at a special ceremony in New York, at the Rescue Workers Memorial at Ground Zero. Since then, as representatives of the many official bodies and volunteer organisations involved in the aftermath of the 9/11 tragedy, Appollo and Peter Davis have remained very much the public faces of a sustained and extraordinarily dedicated mission to heal a shattered city. It is one which remains without parallel in modern times.

Roselle and Salty
Labrador guide dogs
Date of Award: 5 March 2002

For remaining loyally at the side of their blind owners, courageously leading them down more than 70 floors of the World Trade Center and to a place of safety following the terrorist attack on New York on 11 September 2001.

If it is not iniquitous to pick out a single animal to represent the great debt man owes to so many different species, the guide dog is probably the obvious choice. Our reliance on many different animals is enormous – for transport, food, power in some parts of the world and of course companionship – and it is true that not only guide dogs double up as pets and working animals. Even the most mechanised farmers in the most advanced economies will acknowledge that a well-trained sheepdog readily outperforms a quad bike. But there is still something unique about the relationship between a human and his or her canine helper, and it is one which most of us recognise at once.

Of the three dogs recognised by the PDSA at Ground Zero in March 2002, two were guide dogs whose training and extraordinary ability to remain calm and focused enabled them to save the lives of their owners. It must be said also that in a less easily defined way both managed to make a positive impact on those who encountered them on the day.

The first of these, a yellow Labrador called Roselle, belonged to Michael Hingson, a 51-year-old who had been blind since birth and who at 08.45 was already at work in a computer company on the 78th floor of the North Tower. A University of California graduate, Hingson has since likened what turned out to be the impact of the first aircraft 15 storeys above him to a massive earthquake, although it was clear from the choking stench of jet fuel that something else was afoot.

After a quick call to his wife, and aware that the building was in terrible trouble, Hingson decided to make the long descent down the stairs rather than attempting to use one of the lifts. Roselle had been dozing beneath his desk, and grabbing her harness – the two had been partnered for only nine months – he told her it was time to go to work. In fact, he says, she was already set to go and led him through the wreckage of the office towards the stairwell.

While such a descent would be a challenge under any circumstances, the stairs soon became congested and hot with the ambient temperature climbing alarmingly to more than 90 degrees Fahrenheit. In fact above them the temperature was more than 1,000 degrees, the heat from the wreckage of American Airlines Flight 11 feeding into the stairwell each time an office door opened as another person attempted to make their way down to safety.

By the time they reached the 50th floor, which while they didn't yet know it was the level at which United Airlines Flight 175 had slammed into the second tower, both Michael and Roselle were beginning to struggle. Repeatedly jostled by others on the stairs, Michael also became aware that growing numbers of people were heading the wrong way – although it was quickly explained to him that those heading up were actually New York firefighters. As he later observed in countless TV and radio interviews, several of them received claps on the back from those making their way down, but also (from Roselle) the last unconditional love they would ever know.

It was naturally hard not to be concerned about what the firefighters would encounter on the upper floors, but entirely dependent on his dog Michael was also worried about Roselle. With little air circulating in the stairwell, and with their surroundings drenched in jet fumes, she was clearly very thirsty and beginning to pant audibly. Fortunately, after the best part of an hour, the pair made it to the lobby and after 1,453 steps down from the 78th floor the dog was able to slake her thirst with water which had collected from countless fractured pipes. Ten minutes later the two of them managed to escape the building.

At this point Michael and a colleague decided to drive clear of the scene, but at 09.50 they heard the first tower collapsing in what Michael described as 'a metal and concrete waterfall'. The two started running for the subway, Roselle remaining calm and utterly focused despite the sudden rise in noise and the growing panic in the streets around them. A policemen directed both of them into the subway just minutes before another giant roiling cloud of ash, glass, paper and steel filled the air as the second tower collapsed in on itself.

Each and every 9/11 escape was remarkable, but Michael Hingson's struck a particular chord with the public. His life so clearly depended on his dog and, despite routinely running for cover whenever thunder threatened, when it really mattered Roselle had come through for him. The two soon became familiar faces on American TV screens, with Roselle receiving more than 400,000 votes from the public to win 'American Hero Dog of the Year' and Michael Hingson starting a new career as national public affairs director for Guide Dogs for the Blind.

Roselle remained by his side for the next six and a half years until her retirement in 2007, but sadly died in 2011 from complications related to immune-mediated thrombocytopenia, a condition which caused her body to attack her blood platelets. She had been diagnosed with this as long ago as 2004 but had borne it with characteristic stoicism.

*

Another dog to exemplify the teamwork and trust that characterise the working life of a guide dog, Salty – also known as Dorado – belonged to Omar Rivera, a computer systems designer for the New York Port Authority who lost his sight at the age of 28. When the first plane struck, his first thought was to follow the advice being given at the time – to sit tight in his 71st-floor North Tower office – evidently because few if any could conceive of the scale of the tragedy that was beginning to unfold.

It was, he says, Salty who persuaded him otherwise. At first the dog fled, a natural response for any animal in such a situation and with the building swaying perceptibly. He quickly returned to Omar's desk, however, the dog's evident state of anxiety suggesting to his handler that he really needed to get up and get out of the building. Omar admits he was very scared and hesitated over whether to stay or go, but the dog at his feet seemed to know that to remain would be fatal so he put the harness on him and made for the exit. The stairs by this time were completely packed, already very hot, full of smoke and of the sound of individuals screaming and shouting instructions.

People were beginning to panic and the descent was slow with more and more people crowding onto the stairs. A guide dog and its handler need space to move, and as this was increasingly in short supply Omar decided the dog might have a better chance of survival if allowed to go on alone. He slipped Salty's harness, and the dog started down the stairs before turning and making his way back to Omar's side. Feeling a furry nudge against his leg, he says, 'I knew for certain he loved me just as much as I loved him. He was prepared to die in the hope he might save my life.' Omar later told a film crew, 'He was telling me, I am with you. No matter what. You and I together, and that's – no question.'

From the sounds all around the two as they continued their hour-long descent the whole building was clearly about to collapse. Somehow the pair were able to reach ground level before this happened, however, and within a few minutes they were out on the street. As the first building began to come down, they started running, the dog finding a path through the chaos and the literally thousands of other terrified people with Omar holding tightly to his harness.

Omar of course could see nothing of this, but he could 'hear everything . . . a hundred million sounds all concentrated in one place'. People were screaming, the sound of helicopters tore at the air, and sirens sounded repeatedly. Even today, he says, a siren, such a familiar sound in a big modern city, still makes him anxious – and Salty too developed what Omar has described as 'some kind of fear' after the terrible events of that day.

The two remained together for more than ten years. In 2008 Salty was put to sleep, but Omar's love and his admiration for the dog's selfless and heroic character clearly live on still. However, Salty and others like him, he says, 'give everything they have for almost nothing, just for love'. Cynics might say it is just their training, something in their nature, or that such dogs simply did what they did and that is an end to it. But just as it is frequently observed that the worst of humanity can somehow bring out the very best in people, most of us, I am sure, find in the stories of Appollo, Salty and Roselle something extraordinary, something utterly wonderful and something worth celebrating.

The hundreds of firefighters, policemen and -women, dog handlers and other rescue workers at Ground Zero showed enormous endurance in the face of extreme hazard. But ordinary New Yorkers pulled together too, and there was magnificent defiance and great dignity in the way people confronted the disaster by continuing with their daily lives. Panicking might have been a more logical response, or fleeing their city, or simply losing hope. Could they have done it without Appollo and his canine colleagues? Of course to a degree they could have and would have, but no one can say how or indeed how well this might have played out.

Epilogue

In the 1940s, when families in London and other British cities emerged from the shelters to see their houses and workplaces broken and burned, the certainty is that without search dogs many of those injured would not have been rescued in time, nor would the dead have been recovered from the ruins in order to bring comfort and closure to the bereaved. Similarly the men on the front line, and in some cases behind enemy lines, would have fared less well without the companionship provided by the animals whose stories have been told here. Still more of them would have been captured or killed but for the warnings given, the vital messages carried, and even on occasion the assailants attacked by those animals who accompanied them into battle.

In every theatre of war these men and women have showed indomitable courage and fortitude which even now is hard to grasp entirely. But so too did the animals that went with them. Of course there will always be some who question the concept of heroism or bravery in a dog or a cat or a horse or a bird; but more of us find ourselves moved by the animals' stories, and moved to think about what they mean. Many also take great pleasure in seeing the deeds of animals recognised and rewarded in this small but sincere and heartfelt way, and perhaps all one can really say to the doubters is this: read their stories, listen to the people who knew them, and then decide.

Inevitably most PDSA Dickin Medal recipients are now dead, but few if any have been forgotten, and as their stories are told and retold they continue to resonate and to illuminate their lives and our own. In human terms each of them achieved something truly remarkable, and perhaps now they are gone the only hope – to quote the Old Testament prophet Isaiah – is that somewhere in the hereafter 'they will soar on wings like eagles; they will run and not grow weary; they will walk and not be faint'. But most of all, and in a very real sense, it can be said, 'They also served'.

Appendix

The PDSA Gold Medal

With the Dickin Medal traditionally reserved for animals with specified military connections, the decision was taken in 2001 to create a new award for their civilian counterparts. Unsurprisingly, since the first presentation in November the following year, the PDSA Gold Medal has been likened to the George Cross, a comparison which if nothing else underscores how it should not be seen as in any way being inferior to the Dickin Medal.

As with the Dickin Medal, awards are made only very rarely, and at the time of writing a mere 20 medals have been struck in the course of more than a decade. To be considered, animals must be shown to have demonstrated considerable initiative and exceptional devotion to duty in truly exceptional circumstances. Chiefly this means those situations where the animal has saved a human life or lives, and very often to have done so at significant risk to its own safety and well-being.

Gold Medals have also been awarded posthumously to a number of animals in public service, such as police or rescue dogs. In such cases, in the face of armed or violent opposition, the animal has died at the scene or as a result of injuries sustained at the scene.

Bulla, GM
Leicestershire Police
Date of posthumous Award: 13 November 2002
For displaying outstanding gallantry in the line of police duty, and in the face of violent opposition.

Bulla, an Alsatian serving with the Leicestershire Constabulary, was killed in the line of duty in May 1990 while helping his handler apprehend a man brandishing a butcher's knife. The man was threatening both civilians and police officers, and when Bulla and his handler Leigh George intervened the dog was stabbed through the neck and into the heart. Despite all efforts to save him, Bulla died at the scene. PC George (now retired) received the award on his behalf from HRH Princess Alexandra in her role as PDSA patron.

Metpol Delta Monty, GM
Metropolitan Police
Date of Award: 13 November 2002
For displaying outstanding gallantry, despite serious injuries, while carrying out official duties in the face of violent opposition.

Serving in London with the Metropolitan Police, Monty's award was made in recognition of his gallantry following an armed siege in the capital.

In February 2001 Monty, a German shepherd, was instrumental in overpowering a man wielding a knife and threatening his handler, PS Stuart Judd. Monty was stabbed several times but continued to do his duty and following emergency surgery was able to return to duty six weeks later.

Endal, GM
Canine Partner
Date of Award: 13 November 2002
For saving the life of his owner, Allen Parton, through exceptional devotion to duty.

Endal, the canine partner of Gulf War veteran Allen Parton, was awarded the PDSA Gold Medal in recognition of his remarkable skills as well as his outstanding abilities as a companion and an unstinting devotion to duty.

When the Royal Navy officer suffered brain injuries in an accident during the 1991 Gulf War, he was left unable to walk, talk, read or write. A chance introduction to the Labrador retriever literally changed his life, the dog becoming both the inspiration he needed and the motivation for his eventual rehabilitation. As his owner's partner around the home, on the street and at work, the dog rekindled Allen's enthusiasm for life.

May 2001 saw a characteristic but outstanding act of devotion when Allen was knocked out of his wheelchair in a hotel car park and left unconscious. Endal did not panic but calmly manoeuvred Allen into the recovery position, covered him with a blanket from the wheelchair and then pushed his mobile phone towards Allen's face. Only when Allen regained consciousness did Endal leave his side to summon help.

Orca, GM
Canine Partner
Date of Award: 5 April 2006

For saving the life of his owner, Cheryl Alexander, through exceptional devotion to duty.

On 18 May 2003 university student Cheryl Alexander and her golden retriever were enjoying an afternoon in the countryside near Heslington, Yorkshire. With Cheryl for just five weeks, Orca was running alongside her wheelchair, something he loved to do.

The powered wheelchair hit a rock on the pathway and pitched Cheryl down a 15-foot embankment into a water-filled ditch. The wheelchair followed, landing directly on top of Cheryl, who was pinned partially face down in water and unable to move.

Instructed by his owner to get help, Orca was at first mistaken for a lost dog and put on a lead. Breaking free of the collar he ran on, eventually leading a friend and neighbour of Cheryl's back to the ditch. The Fire Brigade was called, an officer subsequently confirming that Orca's remarkable skills and unstinting devotion had saved Cheryl's life.

Blue, GM
West Yorkshire Police
Date of Award: 5 April 2006

For displaying outstanding gallantry, despite serious injuries, while carrying out official duties in the face of violent opposition.

On 8 March 2005 police dog Blue and his handler PC David Proctor were called to assist in the search of a wooded area near

Wakefield, Yorkshire for a violent suspect who was wanted for theft.

Blue quickly located the suspect but after being attacked with a knife sustained appalling injuries. Despite these he followed the man to his hideout and stood guard until his police colleagues arrived, disarmed the man and put him into a secure vehicle.

Blue's injuries included two deep stab wounds to his left shoulder, but he never wavered from his duties until he felt able to stand down. His actions on the day resulted in the detention of an armed offender and the resolution of a very volatile situation which could otherwise have resulted in the loss of human life.

Zoltan, GM
Cleveland Police
Date of Award: 5 April 2006

For displaying outstanding gallantry, despite serious injuries, while carrying out official duties in the face of violent opposition.

On 14 April 2005 Zoltan and his handler Cleveland PC Andrew Lawton were called to join an armed response unit at the scene of an incident in Stockton. A man was threatening police officers and members of the public with a knife.

Officers repeatedly attempted to calm the situation and disarm the man before deploying Zoltan. The police dog's determined efforts were very effective but resulted in Zoltan receiving a stab wound to the chest. The distraction the dog created resulted in the assailant being disarmed and taken into custody.

Zoltan underwent emergency surgery to repair two damaged arteries and a severed chest muscle and to stitch an eight-inch wound. During the operation he lost one fifth of his blood but went on to make a full recovery and subsequently returned to active duty.

Bamse, GM
WWII shop's mascot
Date of posthumous Award: 22 July 2006
For saving the life of two members of the crew of the Royal Norwegian Navy minesweeper, *The Thorodd*, and for his unstinting devotion to duty as ship's mascot during WWII.

This 14-stone St Bernard saved the lives of two members of the crew of the *Thorodd*, a civilian ship drafted into the Royal Norwegian Navy as a coastal patrol vessel in the early stages of World War II.

In the winter of 1941, while the ship was docked at Dundee, Lieutenant Commander O. A. J. Nilsen was set upon by a local man wielding a knife. Bamse immediately rushed the assailant, knocking him into the water. Witnesses confirmed that it was Bamse's decisive and effective action that saved Lieutenant Commander Nilsen's life.

With their homeland overrun by the Nazis, the dog – the name means Teddy Bear – became a symbol for the Norwegian resistance and the Free Norwegian Forces. Wearing his trademark tin helmet, Bamse was frequently photographed in his favourite position by the forward gun turret of the makeshift minesweeper.

In 1942, when the ship was again docked in Dundee, Bamse witnessed a sailor falling overboard and attempted to alert other crew members by barking. No help arrived so, overcoming his known fear of heights, Bamse jumped into the water, swam to the sailor and pulled him to safety.

A loyal mascot, Bamse continued in his duties but died in

July 1944 and is buried in the dunes outside Montrose. His award was made posthumously in 2006 when a large bronze was unveiled by HRH Duke of York in Wharf Street, Montrose. It was positioned facing the dog's birthplace, Honningsvåg in Norway, where an identical statue gazes back towards Bamse's wartime friends in Angus.

Dylan and Cracker, GM
NI Search and Rescue Dog Association
Date of Awards: 27 June 2006

For displaying outstanding gallantry and devotion to duty, while carrying out official duties with the Northern Ireland Search and Rescue Dog Association.

Two golden Labrador retriever brothers attached to the Northern Ireland Search and Rescue Dog Association (SARDA), Dylan and Cracker accompanied by their handler Neil Powell received their awards at a special ceremony held at Belfast Castle.

In March 1999 Dylan was credited with saving the lives of four students lost for several hours high in the Mountains of Mourne during a Duke of Edinburgh Award Scheme exercise. Despite exceptionally poor weather and horrendous conditions, Dylan located the group stranded on a ledge 250 feet from safety, and remained there until the rescue team was able to lift everyone down.

In November of the same year, following the massive Gölcük earthquake in Turkey, Dylan worked in Duzce as part of the UK Fire Service Search and Rescue team and the International Rescue Corps. Following the 7.6 Richter-scale quake which killed in excess of 17,000 people, he located a number of individuals buried alive in the rubble after crawling between floors, climbing ladders and crossing high above dangerous voids.

Dylan's brother Cracker was also in Turkey at this time, demonstrating an outstanding ability to locate casualties deep under the rubble. At the time he was also the only dog in the United Kingdom trained to locate bodies in water, and having done so on at least four occasions has given bereaved families the opportunity to pay their last respects to loved ones.

Vinnie, GM
British Transport Police
Date of Award: 3 July 2007
For gallantry in the service of humanity, immediately following the terrorist attacks on London on Thursday 7 July 2005.

An explosives search dog with British Transport Police, Labrador Vinnie and his handler PC Dave Coleman were on duty in the City of London in July 2005 when they were urgently deployed to the terrorist explosion at Russell Square Tube Station. Vinnie immediately began a search for secondary explosive devices in order to establish a clear and safe route for medical assistance to reach the many casualties.

Overcoming choking smoke and poor visibility, Vinnie then searched the mile-long Underground route from Russell Square to the bomb-damaged train at King's Cross, and completed a reoccupation search of King's Cross Station.

Despite the horrendous devastation and human trauma, Vinnie did not hesitate in carrying out his duties. His skills and tireless devotion to duty were instrumental in restoring public safety and he proved invaluable throughout this tragic event.

Hubble Keck (Jake), GM
Metropolitan Police
Date of Award: 3 July 2007
For gallantry in the service of humanity, immediately following the terrorist attacks on London on Thursday 7 July 2005.

On the same day another explosives search dog, Hubble Keck, a spaniel affectionately known as Jake, was deployed to Tavistock Square with his Metropolitan Police handler PC Robert Crawford. At the scene they found many casualties needing urgent attention after a bomb explosion on a double-decker bus.

Jake immediately began a search of the streets around the blast area, PC Crawford being concerned that there might be a second device. Working amid shattered glass and twisted metal, he secured a safe route for an explosives officer to investigate a suspect device on the bus and for paramedics to reach injured passengers. Jake also then helped secure an area close to the bus where a makeshift field hospital was able to treat casualties.

One of 14 dog active in the area, Jake was later redeployed to search the mile-long Underground route from Russell Square to the bomb-damaged train at King's Cross, and then to search through the wrecked train. Despite significant danger, Jake worked tirelessly and remained undaunted by the work asked of him. His skill, control and unstinting devotion to duty protected members of the public and the emergency services from harm, and his presence and that of PC Crawford proved invaluable throughout this tragic event.

Billy, GM
City of London Police
Date of Award: 3 July 2007
For gallantry in the service of humanity, immediately following the terrorist attacks on London on Thursday 7 July 2005.

Again on the same day, Billy and his handler, City of London PC Rob Brydon-Brown, were deployed to what they initially believed to be a train crash at Aldgate Underground Station. The Labrador was met by a mass of casualties, and from the nature of the injuries it was clear that there had in fact been an explosion.

Billy was tasked to secure the scene by searching the length of the Underground tunnel. Despite immense heat, noise from injured and panicking passengers and very poor visibility, Billy remained constant to his duties and did not falter.

Billy remained on call throughout the day and attended 21 different locations in response to new alerts from the public. Working tirelessly and in the face of danger, his skills and determination to protect the public and the emergency services proved invaluable throughout this tragic event.

Ghillie, GM
Date of Award: 19 December 2007
For gallantry and lifesaving devotion on 19 December 2005 while out walking near his home in Kirkwall on Orkney.

On the morning of Monday 19 December 2007 this devoted two-year-old springer spaniel was enjoying a morning stroll near Kirkwall, Orkney when his owner's mother, Mrs Mary Wilson, suddenly collapsed.

Seeing her lying unconscious, Ghillie wasted no time in running for help. His constant barking attracted the attention of a team of three engineers from Scottish and Southern Energy. Realising the dog was determined to show them something, Leslie Alexander, Brian Moodie and Sandy Thomson followed Ghillie back along the path to the stricken Mrs Wilson. Quickly transferred to Balfour Hospital, Mrs Wilson made a full recovery, thanks in no small part to the clever young dog's quick thinking and determination to get help.

George, GM
Date of posthumous Award: 11 February 2009

For bravery and devotion when protecting the lives of five children in his home town of Manaia, North Island, New Zealand, when they were threatened by two Pit Bull Terriers.

On Sunday 29 April 2007 this 14-year-old Jack Russell terrier was walking with his neighbour's children near his home in Manaia, New Zealand when they were approached from behind by two pit bull terriers.

The dogs were loose and moving quickly towards one of the younger children. George, who had been walking ahead of the group, turned and faced the pit bulls. He rushed at the two dogs, giving the children a chance to escape, but unfortunately George did not recover from the resulting attack and was eventually put to sleep.

The posthumous award of a PDSA Gold Medal was made by Governor General Anand Satyanand in recognition of George's bravery in the face of danger and his determination to protect the lives of five young children.

Bosnich (Bos), GM
Date of Award: 28 July 2009

For saving the life of 73-year-old Mark Corrie, by keeping him warm and alerting a search and rescue team to Mark's plight, who had gone missing for two days after taking Bos for a walk on Cumbrian Fell, on 12 August 2006.

On Saturday 12 August 2006 73-year-old Mark Corrie took his daughter's dog, Bos or Bosnich, for their regular walk in Gelt Woods near Brampton in Cumbria.

When he failed to return by the expected time, Mark's daughter called the police. For two days police search dogs, a helicopter from RAF Boulmer and up to a hundred volunteers from mountain rescue teams scoured the district but without success. Fortunately four local residents decided to investigate a dog howling on the south side of Cumrew Fell, some seven miles away, and at the top of a ridge spotted the black Labrador-cross, who on being seen started barking.

Allowing themselves to be led by the dog, the four found Mark Corrie lying in a concealed spot – cold, confused, suffering from serious dehydration but miraculously unhurt. Bos stayed at his side until Mr Corrie was recovered by the Penrith Mountain Rescue Team and an air ambulance. A paramedic said that without the dog keeping the pensioner warm and alerting the residents Mark Corrie might not have been found in time to save him.

Anya, GM
Wiltshire Police
Date of Award: 6 July 2010
For devotion to duty and lifesaving bravery in the face of danger, when faced with a knife-wielding assailant, on Thursday 3 January 2008.

A police dog who sustained serious stab wounds to the chest while protecting her handler, Anya was on patrol in Swindon in Wiltshire in January 2008 when she and PC Neil Sampson were called to an incident. During the incident PC Sampson was stabbed seven times by an assailant but survived to make a full recovery, in part because the dog was able to hold his attacker down until back-up arrived.

Frodo, GM
Date of Award: 6 July 2010
For lifesaving bravery and determined devotion to his owner and family, when alerting them to a house fire on Friday 13 June 2008.

In May the same year this five-year-old beagle immediately sensed danger when fire broke out in his owners' house at St Bees, Cumbria. In the absence of working smoke alarms the dog barked until David and Jenny Barwise awoke to the danger, and then led the family to safety out of the smoke-filled house.

Oi, GM
Date of posthumous Award: 6 July 2010
For lifesaving bravery and courageous devotion to her family in the face of armed assailants on 18 June 2008.

*

Anya and Frodo were awarded their Gold Medals during a ceremony at the Tower of London in July 2010. A third medal was presented on the same day, but sadly this was another posthumous award, this time going to a Staffordshire bull terrier who had courageously fought off armed intruders during a violent struggle at her owners' home in London in June 2008.

While Oi succeeding in driving the gang off – later identified as four men, some armed with machetes – one member of the family was wounded and Oi received a serious blow to the skull exposing her brain. She received emergency treatment at a PDSA PetAid hospital and recovered only to die of cancer in March 2010.

Dexter, GM
Date of Award: 16 April 2005
For displaying outstanding gallantry, despite serious injuries, while carrying out official duties in the face of violent opposition.

On 20 October 2004 police in Cheltenham received a report of a man threatening shop staff with a knife. An officer was deployed to the scene as the man made his way out of the store brandishing the knife at members of the public. Pursued by police, the man ran through the town, intentionally striking out at a police vehicle with the knife. It was at this point that Dexter was deployed by his handler PC Mark Duncton. As the dog approached, the man slashed him twice in the face with the knife but Dexter continued his pursuit. As a result of Dexter's determination, despite suffering deep lacerations to his muzzle and above his right eye, the offender eventually dropped the knife and was taken into custody.

This was Dexter's first real deployment. Despite the shock of being stabbed twice in the face, he proceeded as he had been trained to do. Dexter's actions resulted in the detention of an armed offender and defused a volatile situation that could have resulted in the loss of human life.

Ellie & Jones, GM
Date of Award: 31 October 2012
For saving the life of their owner through exceptional devotion to duty.

On 10 November 2010 Les Parsons, a Type-1 diabetic from Bridgwater in Somerset, was walking his young German shepherds, Ellie and Jones, when his blood glucose level dropped alarmingly. Unable to take evasive action, or to telephone for help, Les collapsed into semi-consciousness whilst attempting to get to safety. Ellie waited by her owner, licking his face to keep him awake, while Jones ran back to the house to raise the alarm.

Unable to gain entry to the family home, Jones raised the alarm by running back and forth until, sensing that something was wrong, Joanna Parsons and her daughter Fiona realised something was amiss. An ambulance was quickly in attendance and Les was fortunately brought out of his diabetic coma and treated at the local hospital for hypothermia.

List of Illustrations

Index

Signal Corps Pigeon Breeding and Training Centre 38
XIX Corps 32
United States Army Air Forces (USAAF) 183
United States Army Communications and Electronics Museum 39
Universal Carrier *see* Bren Universal Carrier
University of Hull 129
Upstart (horse) 216–19
US Navy
  Marine Mammal Programme 76

V-1 flying bomb 124, 182, 190–1, 196, 213, 215–20
V-2 rockets 124, 182, 187, 190–1, 196, 221
Valiant 26
van Oorschot, Maj. Gen. Johan Willem 36
Van Warwyck, SS 5
Vaughan, Flying Officer R.W.G. 106
Vickers Wellingtons 113, 118
Victoria Cross xii, 24, 48, 98, 105, 113, 155, 160
Vinnie (dog) 248
Volunteer Defence Corps 96
von Model, Field Marshal Walther 31, 32

Wake, Nancy 151
Walker, Rifleman Thomas 9
Walker, Robyn 95
War Dog Training School 59, 77, 80, 81, 85, 161
War Office xi, 21, 33, 39, 83, 156, 157, 159
Ward, Lilias 184, 185
Ward, Rowland 31
Wardle, Corp. C. 183–4
Warner, Sir Edward 192
Waugh, Evelyn 215
Wavell, Archibald Percival, 1st Earl Wavell 91
Westland Lysander 125, 129
Whale Island Gunnery School 2
White Cross of St Giles 7
White Vision (pigeon) 104–107, *105*

Whittle, Gordon 54
William of Orange (pigeon) 47–50
Williams, Doris 8
Williams, Leading Aircraftman Frank 4–8
Williams, Lt-Col. E.A.W. 10
Wilson, Mary 250
Windred Snr, Edward Henry 31, 33
Wings for Victory appeal 42
Winkie (pigeon) 101–104
Winnipeg Grenadiers 95
Wolverton Express 109
Women's Auxiliary Police Corps 211
Wood, Sir Howard Kingsley 42
Wootton Bassett 65
World Trade Center 222–7, 227–31
World War I 2, 20, 59, 130, 134, 173, 209
  First Battle of the Marne 20
World War II xi, 19, 20–22, 75, 99–101, 199–207
  Baedecker raids 139–41
  Battle of Hong Kong 96–8
  Battle of Lye Mun 95–8
  Battle of Sedjenane 77–8
  Battle of the Atlantic 100, 101–4, 104–7, 133, 136-8
  Battle of the Coral Sea 51, 93
  Battle of the Ruhr 118
  Battle of the Scheldt 81-3
  Blitz 174–98, 211–21, 239
  Bombing of Cologne 117–19
  Burma 124, 210
  Crete 154–6
  Czechoslovakia 88–91
  D-Day 25, 26–30, 44–6, 55–6, 59, 86, 123, 130, 131
  Denmark 151–53
  Dieppe raid 22–6
  Dunkirk 76
  French resistance 128, 148, 150–1
  Huon Gulf 50–4
  Italy 10–11, 36–9, 79–80, 108, 122, 157, 159
  Japanese prison camps 3–8
  Kokoda Trail 93
  Malayan Campaign 3, 124, 167
  Manus Island 91, 93
  Mediterranean 108–10